E S T A T E   P U B L

BASINGSTOKE
ANDOVER

ALTON · HEATH END · KINGSCLERE
OAKLEY · OVERTON · TADLEY
WHITCHURCH

GW00371665

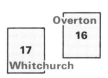

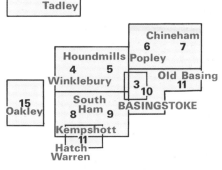

Heath End
12   13
        Tadley

Kingsclere
    14

Chineham
6   7
Popley

Houndmills
4   5
Winklebury

Old Basing
11

3
10

Overton
16

15
Oakley

South
Ham
8   9
BASINGSTOKE

17
Whitchurch

Kempshott
11

Hatch
Warren

Penton
Mewsey
20   21
Charlton

Knights Enham
22   23
Walworth

ANDOVER
26   27

24   25
Anna Valley

18   19
ALTON

Every effort has been made to verify the accuracy of information in this book but the publishers cannot accept responsibility for expense or loss caused by any error or omission. Information that will be of assistance to the user of the maps will be welcomed.

The representation of a road, track or footpath on the maps in this atlas is no evidence of the existence of a right of way.

One-way Street	→
Car Park	🅿
Place of Worship	+
Post Office	●
Public Convenience	Ⓒ
Pedestrianized	▨

Scale of street plans: 4 inches to 1 mile
Unless otherwise stated

Street plans prepared and published by ESTATE PUBLICATIONS, Bridewell House, TENTERDEN, KENT, and based upon the ORDNANCE SURVEY mapping with the permission of The Controller of H. M. Stationery Office.

The publishers acknowledge the co-operation of the local authorities of towns represented in this atlas.

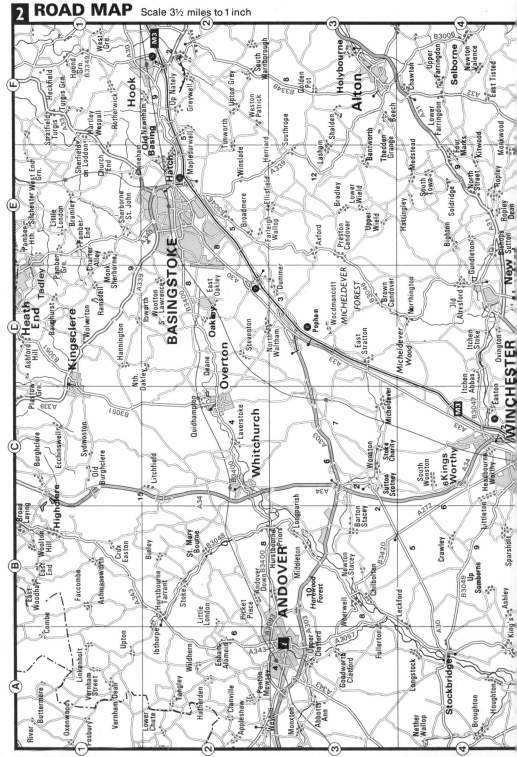

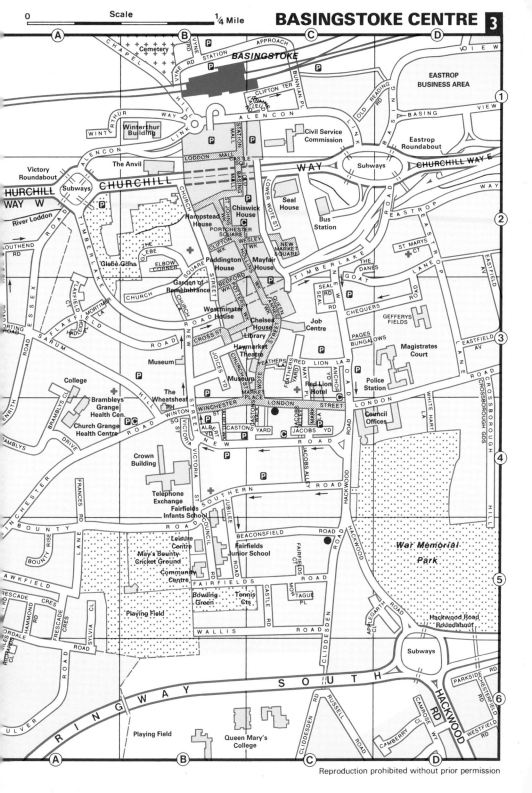

BASINGSTOKE CENTRE 3

Scale 0 — 1/4 Mile

4 WINKLEBURY

Golf Course

Wootton St Lawrence
Manor Farm

Wooton Copse

Worting Wood

Wortingwood Farm

Rooksdown
School

Nightingale Gds
Nightingale Av
Billiesdorn
Gander Dr
Rooksdown
Barron
Mill Road
Vitellius Gds
Julius Cl

ROAD
WELLINGTON
B. Caesar
Claudius
Augustus Way
Hadrians
Tiberius
Waterloo
Dunsford
Rose Hodson Pl
Arundel Gds
Beech
Firs Way
Restormel Way
Oaklands
Elmwood
Hawthorn
Kenilworth Cl
Carls Cl
Blackdam Way
Pendennis Cl
Tintagel Rd
Fort Hill Community School

KENILWORTH

Winklebury

Westgate Cl
Hillcrest Cl
Three Barrels PH
Winklebur Centre
Castle Hill Junior & Infant Schools
June Cl
Dudley
Winklebury
Greenbury Rd
Hertford Rd
Way
Portway Pl
Pembroke
Hastings
ROAD
Wayside
Tiverton Rd
Westfield Lido
Putting Green
Golf Driving Range

Worting
Worting House
Worting Park
Roman Way
Becket
Wykeham Dr
R. Bonel
Aylings Cl
Dorchester
Moniton Trading Estate
West Ham Lane

Scrapps Hill Farm
B3400
WORTING ROAD

ROMAN WAY
BECKET CL
GLEBE LA
CHURCH LA
Rec Grd
Cricket Ground
Kempshott
Cotswold Cl
Chilton Way
Glebe
Worting Junior & Infant Sch
Victoria
Cairn
Tweed Cl
Hicks Kin
Fiske Cl
Old Worting Road
WORTING

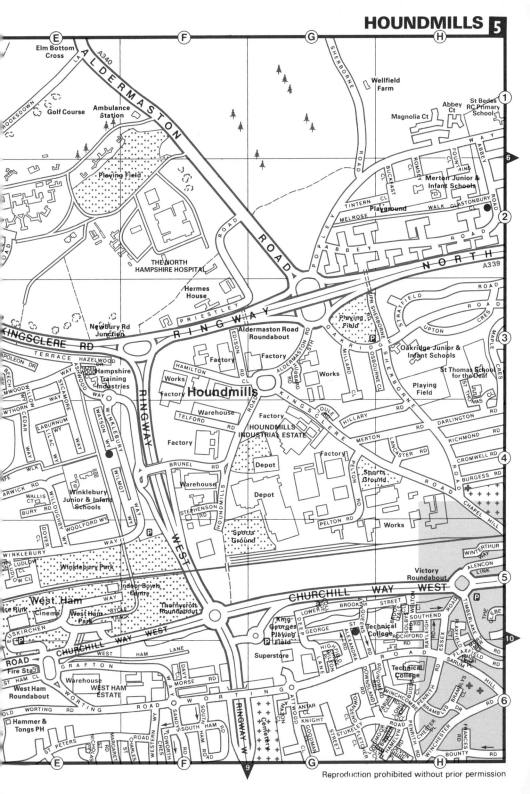

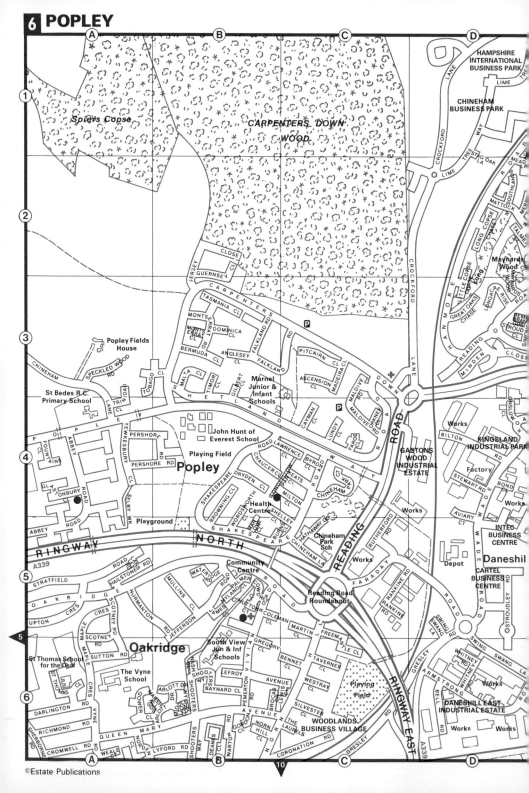

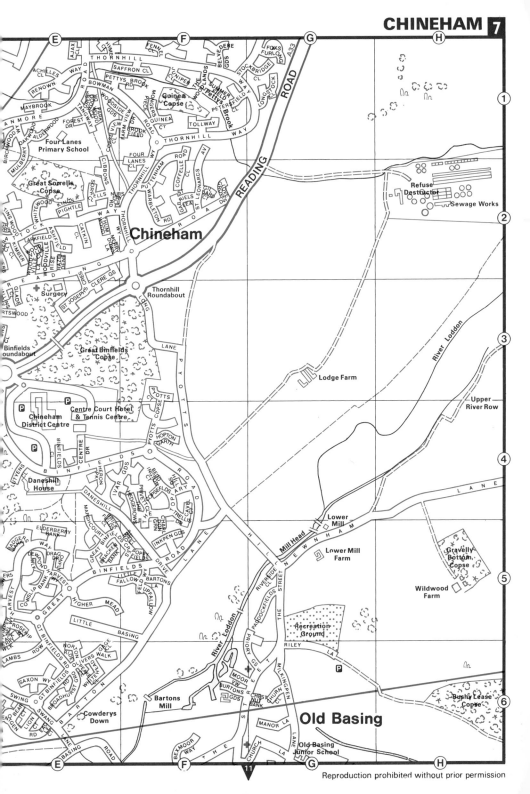

Reproduction prohibited without prior permission

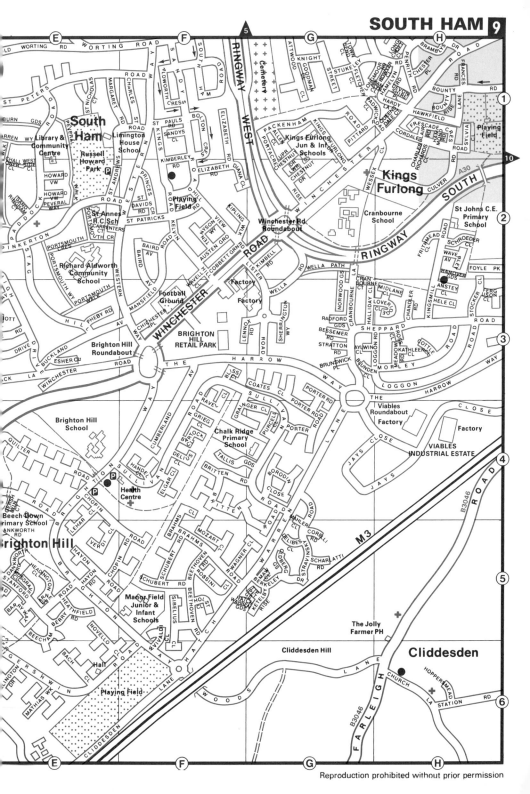

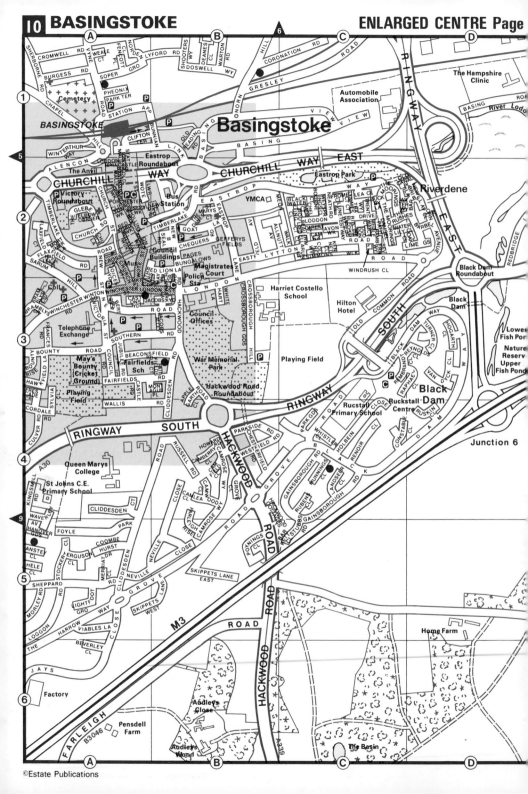

Basingstoke

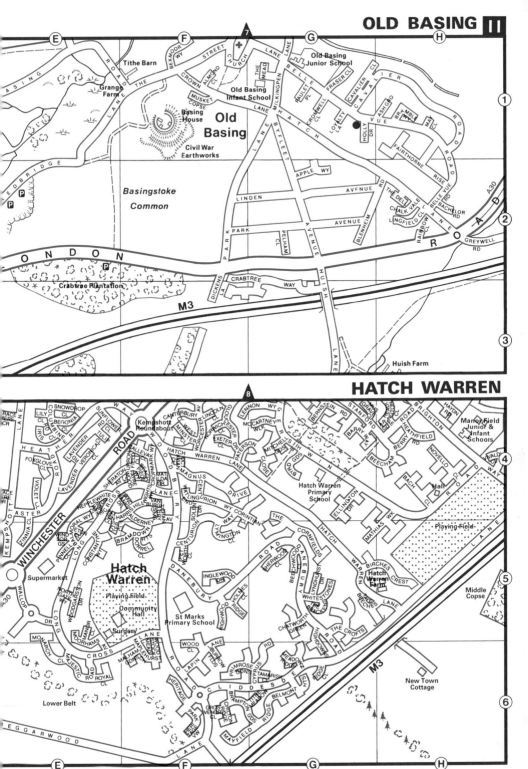

HATCH WARREN

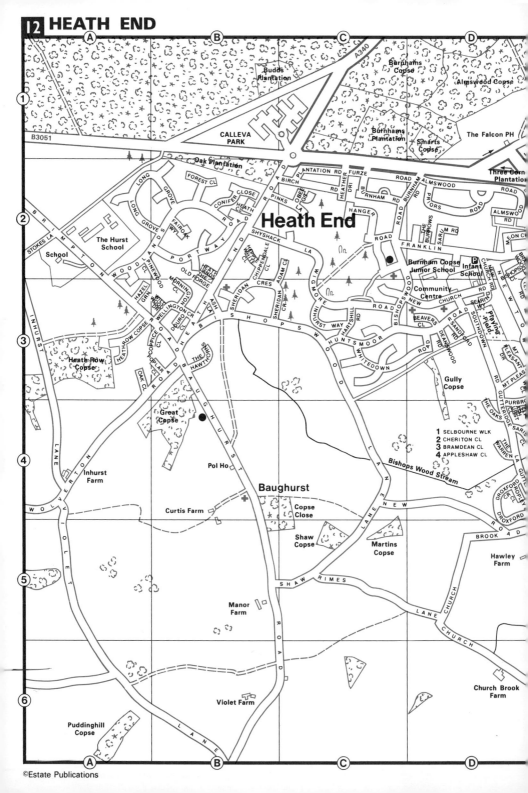

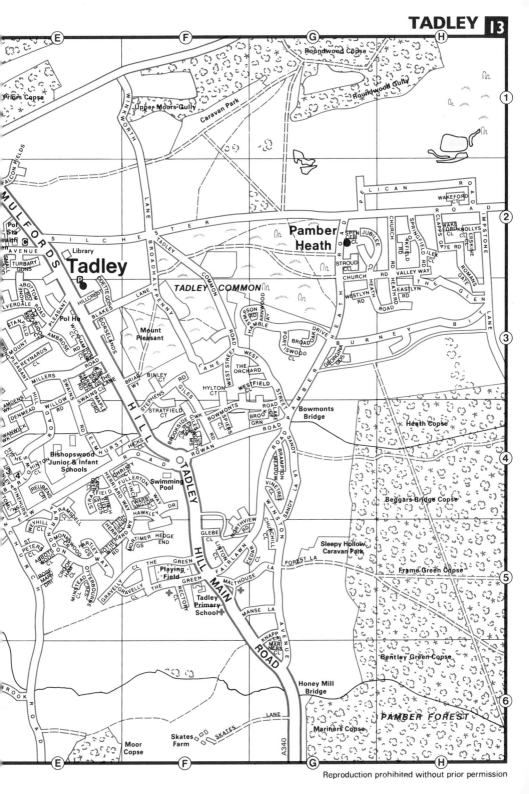

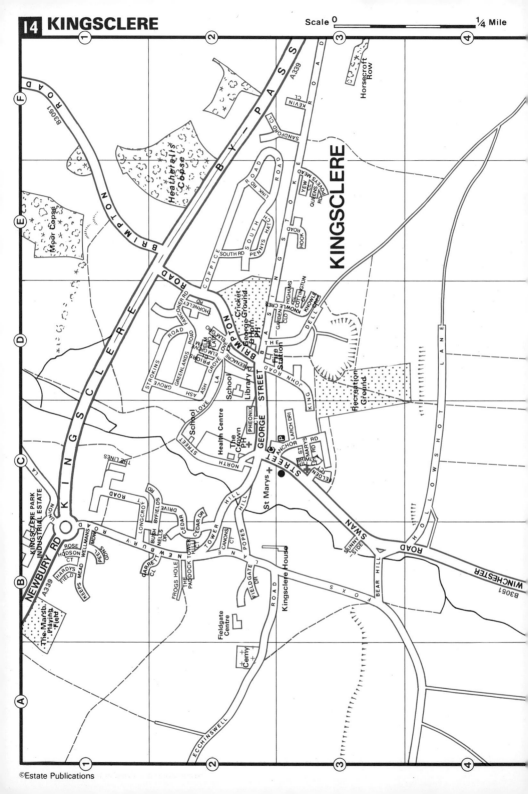

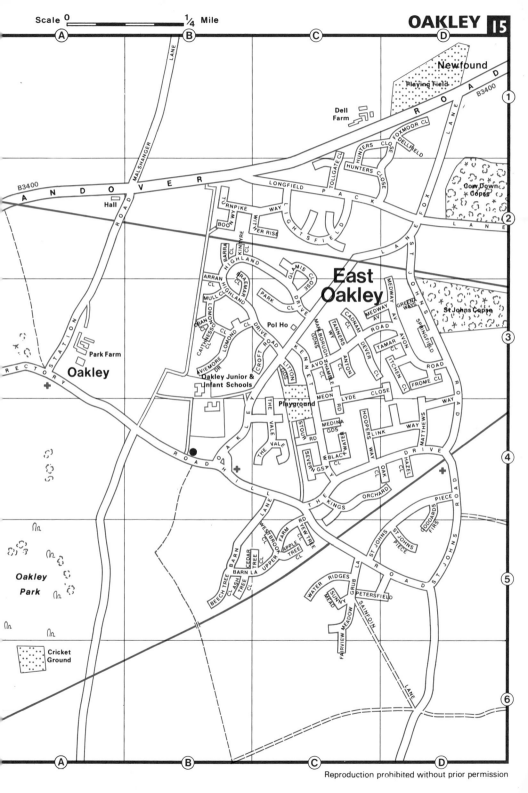

Scale 0 ¼ Mile

A B C D

Newfound

Playing Field

B3400

1

Dell
Farm

FOXMOOR CL

HUNTERS CLOSE

DELLFIELD

TOLLGATE CL

LONGFIELD

HUNTERS CLOSE

PACK

Cow Down
Copse

B3400

A N D O V E R

MALSHANGER

LANE

Hall

ROAD

2

TURNPIKE WAY

WILLMER RISE

BOON CL

HIGHTSFIELD

FOX

LANE

JOHNS

H BARRA CL

KINTYRE CL

HIGHLAND

GLAMIS CLOSE

PARK DRIVE

CL

East
Oakley

MEDWAY

GREENA
WAYS

St Johns Copse

ARRAN CL

BRAEMAR

MULL

HIGHLAND

LOMOND CL

Pol Ho

CADNAM

TANNERS

MEDWAY
AV

AV

ROAD

SPRINGFIELD

3

RECTORY

STATION

Park Farm

OBAN CL

CAITHNESS

LOMOND CL

DRIVE

CROFT ROAD

KENNET

MARLBOROUGH GDNS

ZHAMBLE WY

AVON

ANTON CL

DEVER

TAMAR

AVON

ITCHEN CL

FROME CL

ROAD

Oakley

AVIEMORE DR

Oakley Junior &
Infant Schools

LITTON GDNS

MEON RD

LYDE

CLOSE

WAY

4

THE VALE

Playground

STOUR RD

MEDINA
GDS

WATER

BLACK

HOOPERS WAY

MATTHEWS

WAY

OAK CL

HAZEL CL

DRIVE

THE VALE

SEVEN GS

CL

THE KINGS

ORCHARD

PIECE

St JOHNS

GODDARDS FIRS

ST JOHNS
PIECE

ROAD

BARN

BEECH TREE CL

ASH TREE CL

CEDAR TREE CL

WESTBROOK CL

UPPER FARM RD

APPLE TREE CL

NEW TREE CL

St JOHNS

ROAD

5

Oakley
Park

WATER RIDGES

SUNNY MEAD

GRUB LA

PETERSFIELD

SAINFOIN

LANE

ROAD

FAIRVIEW MEADOW

Cricket
Ground

6

A B C D

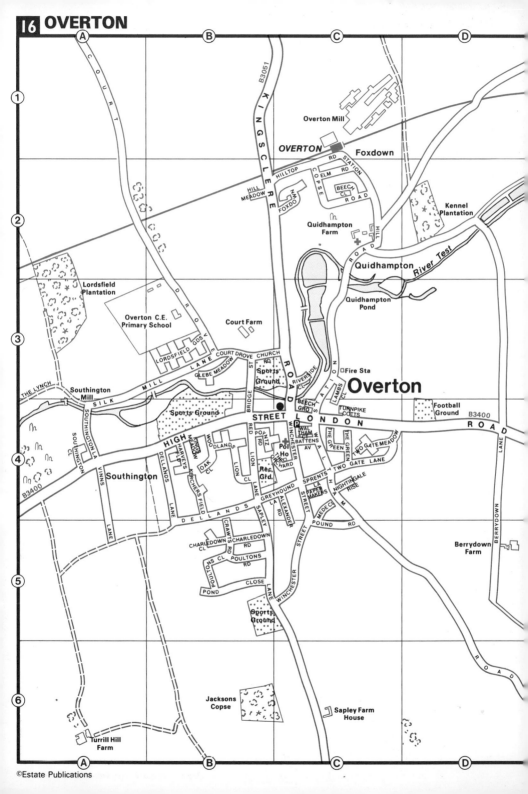

Overton

Overton Mill

OVERTON   Foxdown

Kennel Plantation

Quidhampton Farm

Quidhampton

River Test

Quidhampton Pond

Lordsfield Plantation

Overton C.E. Primary School

Court Farm

Fire Sta

THE LYNCH

Southington Mill

Sports Ground

Sports Ground

Football Ground

B3400

Southington

B3400

Rec. Gfd.

Southington

Charledown

Poultons

Berrydown Farm

Sports Ground

Jacksons Copse

Sapley Farm House

Turrill Hill Farm

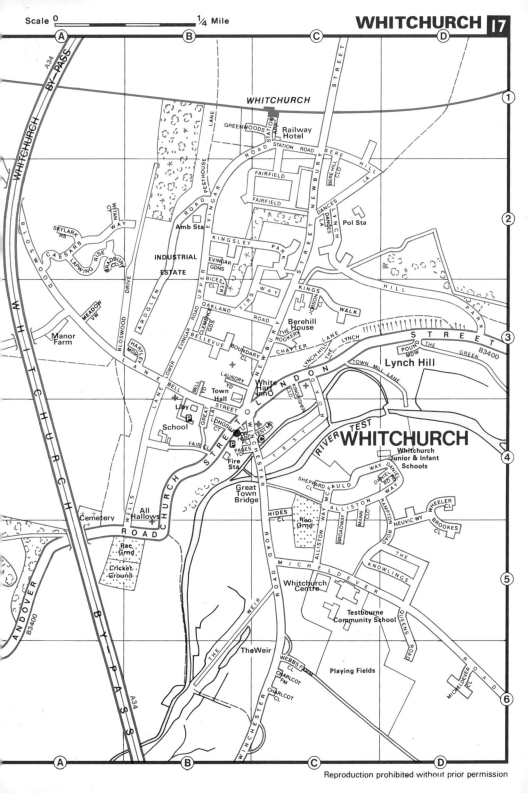

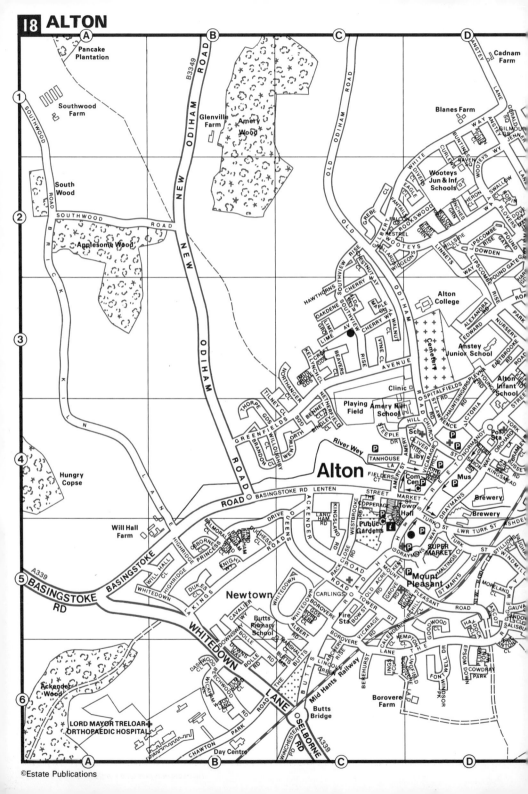

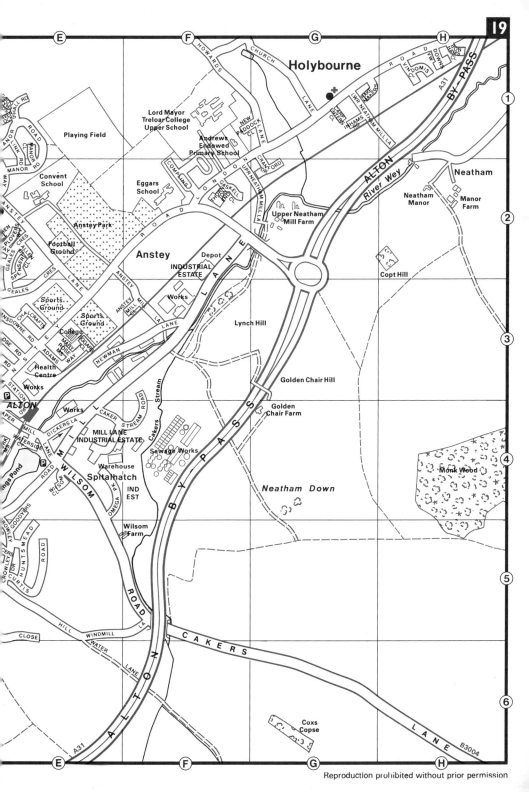

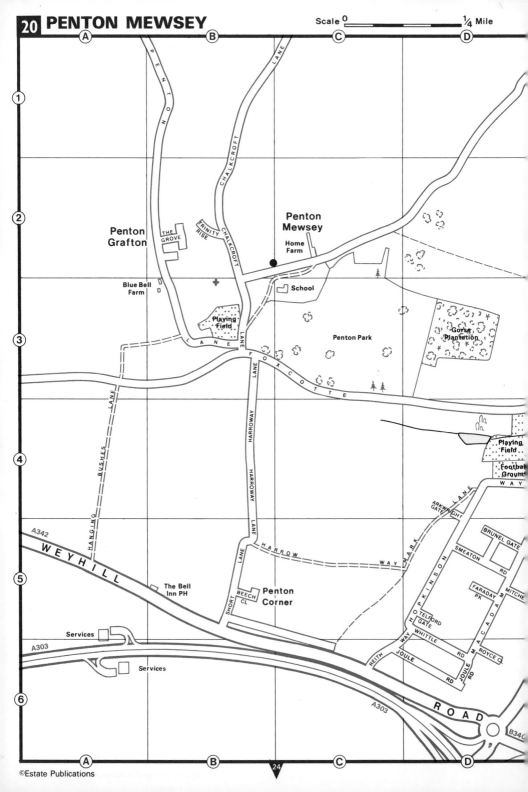

Scale 0 ¼ Mile

Penton
Mewsey

Penton
Grafton

THE GROVE

TRINITY RISE

CHALKCROFT LANE

PENTON LANE

Home Farm

Blue Bell
Farm

School

Playing
Field

Penton Park

Gorse
Plantation

FOXCOTTE LANE

BUSHES LANE

HANGING LANE

HARROWAY

HARROWAY

Playing
Field

Football
Ground

WAY

ARKWRIGHT GATE

MARK LANE

BRUNEL GATE

SMEATON RD

FARADAY PK

MITCHE

A342

WEYHILL

The Bell
Inn PH

SHORT LANE

BEECH CL

Penton
Corner

HARROW WAY

HOPKINSON WAY

TELFORD GATE

WHITTLE RD

JOULE RD

JOULE RD

REITH RD

MACADAM

ROYCE C

Services

A303

Services

A303

ROAD

B340

24

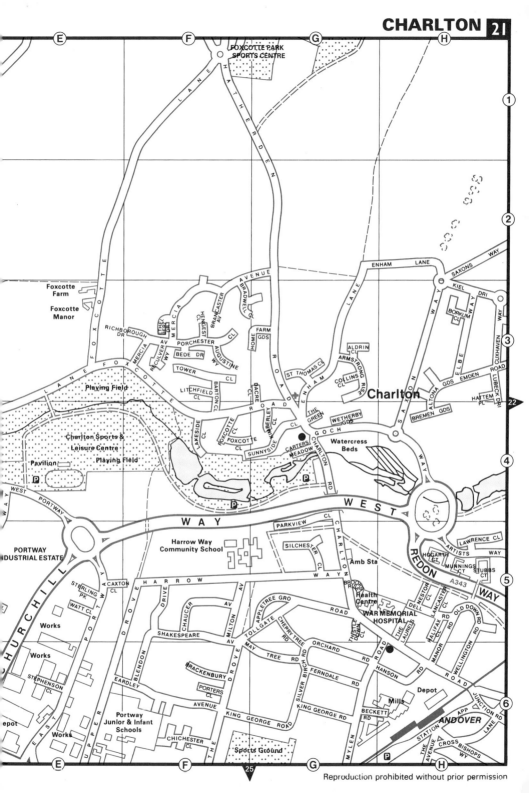

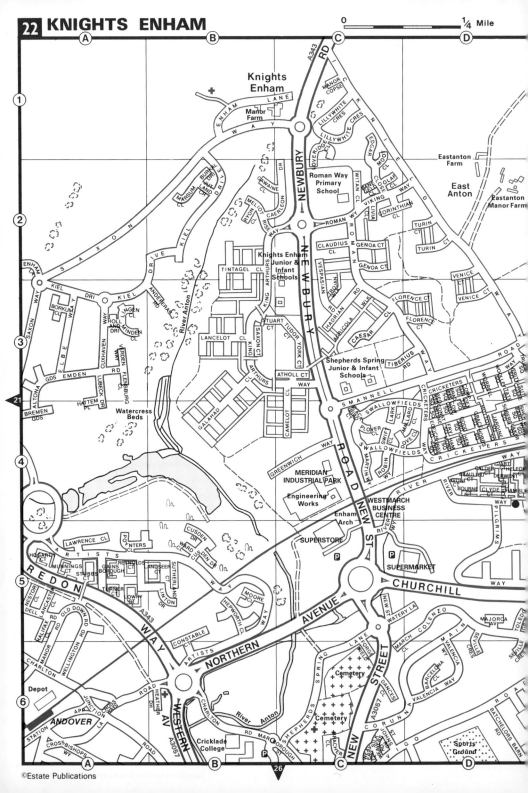

E F G H

1

2

3

Finkley Down
Farm Park

ROAD

4

Works
Works
Depot
Sports Ground
Factory
WALWORTH
INDUSTRIAL ESTATE
Engineering
Works
Factory
The Icknield
School
DROVE

5

RIVER
NENE
HOUSE
THAMES
CT
TRENT TYNE
CT
SEVERN WYE CT
SHANNON
PRINCE
CL
NORTH WAY
NORTH
NORTH
WALWORTH WAY
SOUTH WAY
KINGSWAY
CENTRAL WAY
CENTRAL WAY
SOUTH WAY
SOUTH WAY
WAY
WAY
FLINDERS
CL
Works
Works
Works
Factory

PILGRIMS
WAY
CROWN WY
WEST
WAY
CHURCHILL
WAY
LONDON RD
A3093

Vigo Junior &
Infant Schools
MADRID
RD
VIGO RD
GRANADA
PL
ROAD
BILBAO
VIGO
LONDON ROAD
RODNEY CT
NELSON WK
LOVEY
CT
HOWE
PL
SOMER
CT
MLIN
CT
JERVIS
DRAKE
ADMIRALS WK
LONDON RD
BENBOW
COLLINGWOOD
BEATTY
DUNCAN
FISHER WK
ADMIRALS WK
LONDON RD
Queen
Charlotte PH
LONDON RD
MAGELLAN
CL
COLUMBUS WAY
DOUGHTY
SCOTT CT
LIVINGSTONE
CL
LONDON
OX
B3400
ROAD

6

Factory

The Norman
ate School

Playing Field

E F G H

27

Scale 0 ¼ Mile

A
B
C
D

1
2
3
4
5
6

WEYHILL
ROAD

A342
A303
A343

MONXTON R
GALLOWS

SALMOND ROAD
DOUGLAS ROAD
TRENCHARD RD
ELLINGTON CL
TEDDER CL
PORTAL CL
SALMOND ROAD
SLESSOR CL

L.E.A. ANDOVER

Rifle
Range

RED POST LANE

MONXTON

NEWALL RD
DURSTON
DICKSON RD
CLOSE
PATTINSON CRES
HARRIS

Government
Offices

Red Post
Bridge

ROAD

ANDOVER

Glasshouses

Little Park
Farm

Glasshouses

Glasshouses

Glasshouses

Glasshouses

POST LANE

Glasshouses

Glasshouses

Little
Park

Glasshouses

Glasshouses

Glasshouses

CATTLE LANE

Watercress Beds

Glasshouses

Glasshouses

Glasshouses

LANE

CATTLE LANE

Little Ann
Bridge

SALISBURY

LANE

GLEBE MEAD CL

A343

HILLSIDE

DUCK ST

**Abbotts
Ann**

Pillhill Brook

©Estate Publications

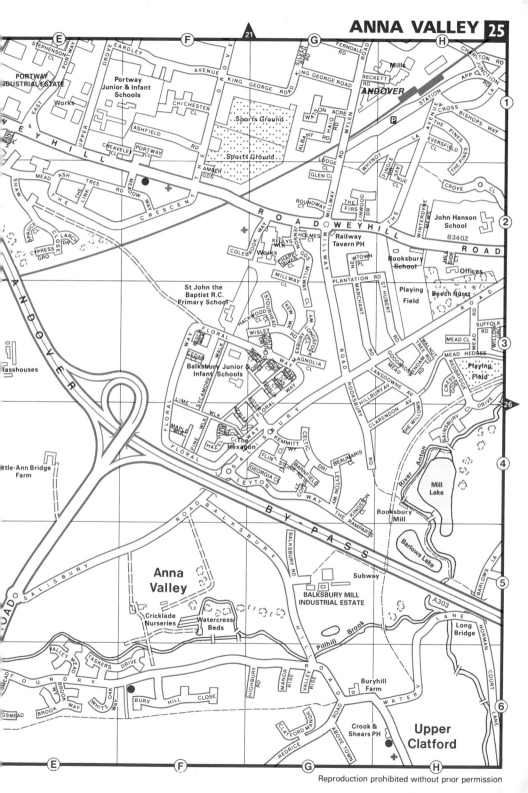

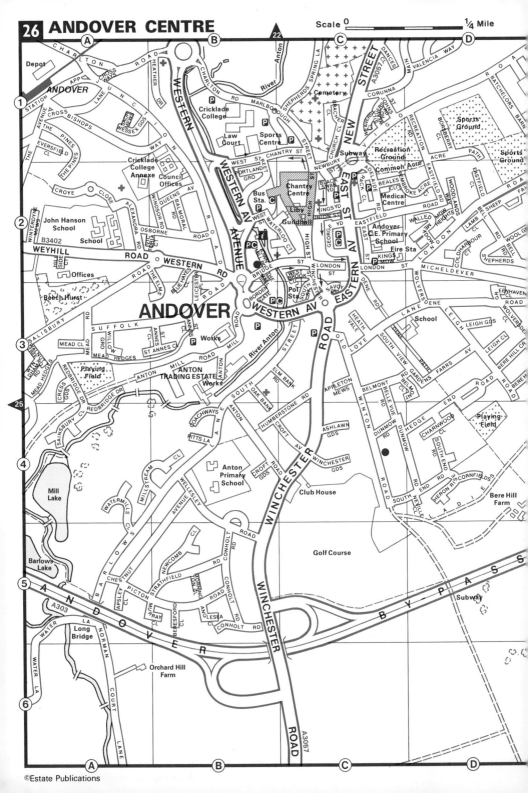

Ellington Clo. SP11 24 D2
Elm Bank Rd. SP10 26 B3
Emden Rd. SP10 21 H3
Enham La. SP10 21 G3
Ethelred Dri. SP10 21 F3
Eversfield Clo. SP10 26 A1
Exbury Way. SP10 25 G3

Faraday Pk. SP10 20 D5
Farrs Av., SP10 26 D3
Ferndale Rd. SP10 21 G6
Fingle Dri. SP10 25 H2
Finkley Rd. SP11 23 F2
Fisher Clo. SP10 27 F1
Flensburg Clo. SP10 22 A3
Flinders Clo. SP10 23 G5
Flint Clo. SP10 25 G4
Floral Way. SP10 25 F2
Florence Ct. SP10 22 C3
Forest La. SP11 27 H4
Forge Field. SP10 22 C6
Forth Ct. SP10 22 D4
Foundry Rd. SP11 25 E6
Foxcotte Clo. SP10 21 F4
Foxcotte La. SP10 20 B3
Foxcotte Rd. SP10 21 E3
Fry Sq. SP10 22 D4

Gainsborough Ct. SP10 22 A5
Galahad Clo. SP10 22 B4
Gallaghers Mead. SP10 24 D1
Gawaine Clo. SP10 22 B2
Genoa Ct. SP10 22 C2
Georges Yard. SP10 26 C2
Georgia Clo. SP10 25 G4
Gilberts Mead Clo. SP11 24 D6
Glen Clo. SP10 25 G2
Goch Way. SP10 21 G4
Goddard Sq. SP10 22 D4
Goddards Mead. SP10 25 H3
Grace Sq. SP10 22 D4
Granada Pl. SP10 23 E5
Graveney Sq. SP10 22 D4
Greenhaven Clo. SP10 26 D3
Greenwich Way. SP10 21 H5

Hackwood Clo. SP10 25 G3
Hadrian Rd. SP10 22 C3
Haig Rd. SP10 25 G1
Halifax Clo. SP10 21 H5
Hamble Ct. SP10 22 D4
*Hamburg Clo, Holland Dri. SP10 22 A3
Hammond Sq. SP10 22 D4
Hanging Bushes La. SP11 20 A5
Hanover Clo. SP10 25 F4
Hanson Rd. SP10 21 H6
Harris Clo. SP11 24 C3
Harrow Way, Andover. SP10 21 F5
Harrow Way, Penton Corner. SP11 20 B5
Harrow Way La. SP11 20 B4
Hawke Clo. SP10 27 F1
Hatherden Rd. SP10 21 F1
Hattem Pl. SP10 21 H3
Hazel Clo. SP10 25 F4
Heath Vale. SP10 26 C3
Heather Dri. SP10 22 B6
Hedge End Rd. SP10 26 D4
Helford Ct. SP10 22 D4
Hendren Sq. SP10 22 D4
Hengest Clo. SP10 21 F3
Hepworth Clo. SP10 22 B5
Heron Rise. SP10 26 D4
High St. SP10 26 C2
Highbury Rd. SP11 25 G6
Highlands Rd. SP10 27 E2
Hillbury Av. SP10 25 G3
Hillside. SP11 24 B6
Hillside Rd. SP10 26 A2
Hobbs Sq. SP10 22 D4
Hogarth Clo. SP10 21 H5
Holland Dri. SP10 22 A3
Holmes Ct. SP10 25 G2
Home Farm Gdns. SP10 21 G3
Hood Clo. SP10 27 F1
Hopkinson Way. SP10 20 D5
Humberstone Rd. SP10 26 B4
Hutton Sq. SP10 22 D4

Icknield Way. SP10 22 C1
INDUSTRIAL ESTATES:
Anton Trading Est. SP10 26 B3

Balksbury Mill Ind Est. SP11 25 G5
Meridian Ind Park. SP10 22 C4
Portway Ind Est. SP10 25 E1
Walworth Ind Est. SP10 23 F5
Westmarch Business Centre. SP10 22 C4

Jardine Sq. SP10 22 D4
Jasmine Ct. SP10 25 G3
Jellicoe Ct. .SP10 23 E6
Jensen Gdns. SP10 25 G2
Jervis Ct. SP10 27 E1
Joule Rd. SP10 20 D6
Junction Rd. SP10 26 A1
Jutland Cres. SP10 22 B2

Kellys Walk. SP10 25 G2
Kemmitt Way. SP10 25 G4
Kennet Ct. SP10 23 E4
Kew Walk. SP10 25 G3
Kiel Dri. SP10 22 A3
Kimberley Clo. SP10 21 G4
King Arthurs Way. SP10 22 B3
King George Rd. SP10 25 F1
Kings Mdw. SP10 26 C2
Kings Yard. SP10 26 C2
Kingsmead. SP11 25 E6
Kingston Clo. SP10 25 G4
Kingsway. SP10 23 G4

Ladies Walk. SP10 26 D4
Laker Sq. SP10 22 D4
Lakeside Clo. SP10 21 F4
Lamb Clo. SP10 26 D2
Lancaster Clo. SP10 21 H5
Lancelot Clo. SP10 22 B3
Landseer Ct. SP10 22 B5
Lansdowne Av. SP10 25 G3
Larch Dri. SP10 25 E2
Larwood Sq. SP10 22 D4
Lavender Ct. SP10 25 G3
Lawrence Clo. SP10 21 H5
Leicester Pl. SP10 26 B3
Leigh Ct. SP10 26 D3
Leigh Gdns. SP10 26 D3
Leigh Rd. SP10 26 D3
Leyton Way. SP10 25 G4
Lillywhite Cres. SP10 22 C1
Lime Walk. SP10 25 F3
Lingen Clo. SP10 22 A3
Linton Dri. SP10 22 B5
Linwood Clo. SP10 25 G2
Litchfield Clo. SP10 21 F3
Little Copse. SP10 25 G4
Livingstone Rd. SP10 23 G6
Lock Sq. SP10 23 E4
Lodge Clo. SP10 25 G2
London Rd. SP10 26 D2
London St. SP10 26 C2
Longstock Clo. SP10 25 G3
Loveridge Clo. SP10 22 C1
Lowry Ct. SP10 22 A5
Lubeck Dri. SP10 21 H3
Lune Ct. SP10 23 E4

Macadam Way. SP10 20 D6
Madrid Rd. SP10 23 E5
Magellan Clo. SP10 23 G6
Magnolia Ct. SP10 25 G3
Majorca Av. SP10 22 D5
Manor Copse. SP10 22 C1
Manor Rise. SP11 25 G6
Manor Road. SP10 21 H6
Maple Walk. SP10 25 F4
March Clo. SP10 22 D5
Marchant Rd. SP10 25 G3
Mark La. SP10 20 D5
Marlborough St. SP10 26 B1
Marshall Sq. SP10 23 E4
Marsum Clo. SP10 22 B5
May Tree Rd. SP10 21 G6
Mead Clo. SP10 26 A3
Mead Hedges. SP10 26 A3
Meadow Heights. SP10 26 D2
Mead Rd. SP10 26 A3
Meadow Way. SP10 25 F2
Medina Ct. SP10 23 E4
Medway Ct. SP10 23 E4
Meliot Rise. SP10 22 B2
Mercia Av. SP10 21 F3
Mersey Ct. SP10 23 E4
Micheldever Rd. SP10 26 D2

Millstream Clo. SP10 26 A4
Millway Clo. SP10 25 G2
Millway Rd. SP10 25 G2
Milton Av. SP10 21 F5
Minden Clo. SP10 22 A3
Mitchell Clo. SP10 20 D5
Monxton Rd. SP10 24 B3
Moore Clo. SP10 22 B5
Moot Clo. SP10 22 C2
Mornington Clo. SP10 26 B5
Mountbatten Ct. SP10 27 E1
Munnings Ct. SP10 21 H5
Murray Clo. SP10 26 A5
Mylen Rd. SP10 25 G1

Napier Walk. SP10 27 E1
Nelson Walk. SP10 27 E1
Nene Ct. SP10 23 E4
Nestor Clo. SP10 21 H5
Neville Clo. SP10 26 D4
New St. SP10 26 C1
Newall Rd. SP11 22 C3
Newbury Rd. SP11 22 C1
Newbury St. SP10 26 C2
Newcombe Clo. SP10 26 B5
Newtown Pl. SP10 25 G2
Norman Court La. SP11 26 A5
North Way. SP10 23 E4
Northern Av. SP10 22 B6

Oak Bank. SP10 26 B3
Olaf Clo. SP10 22 C2
Old Down Rd. SP10 21 H6
Old Winton Rd. SP10 26 C3
*Oldenburg Clo, Lingen Clo. SP10 22 A3
Orchard Rd. SP10 21 G6
Orchid Ct. SP10 25 G3
Osborne Rd. SP10 26 A2
Ouse Ct. SP10 23 E4
Ox Drove. SP11 27 G1

Palmer Dri. SP10 27 E2
Parkview Clo. SP10 22 B5
Pattinson Cres. SP11 24 C3
Pearmain Dri. SP10 27 E2
Pembroke Ct. SP10 26 C2
Pen Clo. SP10 27 E2
Penton La. SP10 20 B1
Picket Twenty. SP11 27 G1
Picton Rd. SP10 26 A5
Pilgrims Way. SP10 22 D4
Pine Walk. SP10 25 F4
Pitts La. SP10 26 B4
Plantation Rd. SP10 22 D4
Porchester Clo. SP10 21 F3
Portal Clo. SP10 24 D2
Porters Clo. SP10 21 F6
Portland Gro. SP10 26 B2
Portway Clo. SP10 25 F1
Poynters Clo. SP10 22 A5
Primrose Ct. SP10 25 G3
Prince Clo. SP10 23 E4

Queens Av. SP10 26 B2

Rack Clo. SP10 26 C2
Recreation Rd. SP10 26 D1
Reculver Way. SP10 21 F3
Red Post La. SP11 24 A2
Redbridge Dri. SP10 26 A3
Redon Way. SP10 21 H5
Redrice Rd. SP11 25 G6
Reith Way. SP10 20 D5
Reynolds Ct. SP10 22 A5
Rhodes Sq. SP10 23 E4
Ribble Ct. SP10 23 E4
Richborough Dri. SP10 21 F3
River Way. SP10 22 C5
Robin Way. SP10 22 C4
Rodney Ct. SP10 23 E4
Roman Way. SP10 22 C2
Rooksbury Rd. SP10 25 G3
Roundway Ct. SP10 25 G2
Royce Clo. SP10 20 D4
Ryon Clo. SP10 22 B2

Sainsbury Clo. SP10 26 A4
St Annes Clo. SP10 26 B3
St Hubert Rd. SP10 25 H3
St Johns Rd. SP10 26 C1
St Thomas Clo. SP10 26 C1
Salisbury Rd. SP10 24 D6
Salmond Rd. SP11 24 D2
Savoy Clo. SP10 26 C3
Saxon Ct. SP10 22 B3

Saxon Way. SP10 21 H3
Scott Clo. SP10 23 G6
Severn Ct. SP10 23 E4
Seville Cres. SP10 22 D5
Shackleton Sq. SP10 23 E4
Shakespeare Av. SP10 21 F5
Shannon Ct. SP10 23 E4
Shaw Clo. SP10 25 E2
Sheep Fair. SP10 26 D2
Shepherds Row. SP10 26 D2
Shepherds Spring La. SP10 26 C1
Sheppard Sq. SP10 22 D4
Shoe Mews. SP10 26 A1
Short La. SP10 20 B5
Sidmouth Rd. SP10 27 E2
Silchester Clo. SP10 21 G5
Silk Weavers Rd. SP10 26 C1
Silver Birch Rd. SP10 25 G1
Slessor Clo. SP10 25 G4
Smannell Rd. SP11 22 C4
Smeaton Rd. SP10 20 D5
Sobers Sq. SP10 22 D4
Somerville Ct. .SP10 27 F1
South End Rd. SP10 26 C4
South St. SP10 26 B3
South View Gdns. SP10 26 C3
South Way. SP10 23 F5
Spey Ct. SP10 23 E4
Springfield Clo. SP10 27 F1
Spruce Clo. SP10 25 E2
Statham Sq. SP10 23 E3
Station App. SP10 26 A1
Stephenson Clo. SP10 21 E6
Sterling Clo. SP10 21 E5
Stiles Dri. SP10 27 E2
Stone Clo. SP10 25 G4
Stourhead Clo. SP10 25 G3
Strathfield Rd. SP10 26 B5
Stuart Ct. SP10 22 C3
Stubbs Ct. SP10 21 H5
Suffolk Rd. SP10 26 A3
Sunnyside Clo. SP10 21 G4
Sutcliffe Sq. SP10 22 D3
Sutherland Ct. SP10 22 B5
Swallowfields. SP10 22 C4
Swift Clo. SP10 22 C4
Sycamore Walk. SP10 25 F4

Taskers Dri. SP11 25 E6
Tate Sq. SP10 22 D3
Tedder Clo. SP11 24 D2
Telford Gate. SP10 20 D5
Test Ct. SP10 23 E4
Thames Ct. SP10 23 E4
The Avenue. SP10 26 A1
The Crescent. SP10 25 E2
The Drove. SP10 25 F2
The Elms. SP10 26 B2
The Firs. SP10 25 G2
The Green. SP10 21 G4
The Grove. SP11 20 B2
The Laurels. SP10 21 H5
The Link. SP10 25 E2
The Mall. SP10 26 C1
The Pines. SP10 26 A1
The Ramparts. SP10 25 G4
The Willows. SP10 25 H4
Thistledown Clo. SP10 21 G5
Tiberius Ct. SP10 22 C3
Tintagel Clo. SP10 22 B2
Toledo Gro. SP10 22 D5
Tollgate Rd. SP10 21 G5
Tovey Ct. SP10 23 F6
Tower Clo. SP10 21 F3
Trenchard Rd. SP11 24 D2
Trent Ct. SP10 23 E4
Trinity Rise. SP11 20 B2
Trojan Walk. SP10 22 C3
Trueman Sq. SP10 22 D3
Tudor Ct. SP10 22 C3
Turin Ct. SP10 22 D2
Turner Ct. SP10 22 A5
Tyne Ct. SP10 23 E4

Upper Drove. SP10 25 E1

Valencia Way. SP10 26 D1
Valley Mead. SP11 25 E6
Valley Rise. SP10 25 G6
Venice Ct. SP10 22 D2
Verden Way. SP10 22 A3
Verity Sq. SP10 27 E1
Vespasian Rd. SP10 22 C3
Victoria Ct. SP10 26 B2
Vigo Rd. SP10 26 C1
Viking Way. SP10 22 C2

Walled Meadow. SP10 26 D2
Walnut Tree Rd. SP10 26 A3
Walworth Clo. SP10 23 E5
Ward Clo. SP10 22 B5
Water La. SP11 26 A6
Waterloo Ct. SP10 26 B2
Watermills Clo. SP10 26 A4
Watery La. SP10 22 C5
Watson Acre. SP10 25 G1
Watt Clo. SP10 21 E5
Weavers Clo. SP10 26 C1
Wellesley Rd. SP10 26 B4
Wellington Rd. SP10 21 H6
Wessex Gdns. SP10 26 A1
West Portway. SP10 21 E4
West St. SP10 26 B1
West Way. SP10 23 F5
Westbrook Clo. SP10 26 C2
Western Av. SP10 26 B1
Western Rd. SP10 26 B2
Wetherby Gdns. SP10 21 G4
Weyhill Rd. SP10 25 C1
White Oak Way. SP11 20 D5
Whittle Rd. SP10 20 D5
Whynot La. SP10 25 H1
Willow Gro. SP10 26 A3
Winchester Gdns. SP10 26 C4
Winchester Rd. SP10 26 B4
Winchester St. SP10 26 C2
Windsor Rd. SP10 26 B2
Winterdyne Mews. SP10 26 A2
Winton Chase. SP10 27 E2
Wisley Rd. SP10 25 G3
Wisteria Ct. SP10 25 G3
Witan Clo. SP10 22 C2
Wolversdene Clo. SP10 26 D3
Wolversdene Gdns. SP10 27 E2
Wolversdene Rd. SP10 26 D2
Woodlands Way. SP10 26 D2
Wool Gro. SP10 26 D2
Woolley Sq. SP10 22 D3
Worrell Sq. SP10 22 D3
Wye Ct. SP10 23 E4
Wyndham Rd. SP10 26 A3

York Ct. SP10 22 C3

BASINGSTOKE

Abbey Ct. RG24 5 H1
Abbey Rd. RG24 5 G2
Abbott Clo. RG22 9 E3
Achilles Clo. RG24 7 E1
Acorn Clo. RG21 10 D2
Aghemund Clo. RG24 6 D1
Ajax Clo. RG24 7 E1
Albert Yd. RG21 3 B4
Albert Wk. RG21 3 B4
Aldermaston Rd. RG24 5 E1
Aldermaston Rd Sth. RG21 5 G3
Alderney Av. RG22 11 F4
*Alders Clo, The Moorings. RG21 10 C2
Alderwood. RG24 7 E1
Aldworth Cres. RG22 9 F1
Alencon Link. RG21 3 B2
Alexandra Rd. RG21 5 G5
Allen Clo. RG21 9 G1
Alliston Clo. RG22 8 D2
Alliston Way. RG22 8 D2
Allnutt Av. RG21 10 B2
Almond Clo. RG24 11 F1
Alpine Ct. RG22 8 C1
Amazon Clo. RG21 5 G6
Amport Clo. RG24 7 F4
Anchor Yard. RG21 3 C3
*Anglers Pl, The Moorings. RG21 10 C2
Anglesey Clo. RG24 6 B3
Anstey Clo. RG21 9 H3
Antar Clo. RG21 5 G6
Antrim Clo. RG22 8 C2
Applegarth Clo. RG21 3 D5
Apple Way. RG22 11 G2
Arlott Dri. RG21 6 B6
Armstrong Rd. RG24 6 D6
Arne Ct. RG22 9 E5
Arun Ct. RG21 10 C2
Arundel Gdns. RG23 4 D3
Ascension Clo. RG24 6 C3
Ash Gro. RG24 11 H1

Ashfield. RG24 7 E3
Ashwood Way. RG23 5 E3
Aster Rd. RG22 8 B6
Attwood Clo. RG21 5 G6
Augustus Dri. RG23 4 D3
Auklet Clo. RG22 8 A5
Austen Gro. RG22 9 F2
Avon Walk. RG21 10 C2
Aylings Clo. RG21 4 C6
Aylwin Clo. RG21 9 G3

Bach Clo. RG22 9 E6
Bachelor Rd. RG24 11 H2
Badgers Bank. RG24 7 E5
Baird Av. RG22 9 F2
Ballard Clo. RG22 8 D1
Balmoral Ct. RG22 8 D2
Balmoral Way. RG22 11 E5
Barbel Av. RG21 10 D2
Bardwell Clo. RG22 8 D1
Barrett Clo. RG21 10 C5
Barron Pl. RG24 4 D2
Barry Way. RG22 9 E5
Bartock Clo. RG22 9 F4
Barton La. RG24 7 E6
Bartons La. RG24 7 F5
Basing Rd. RG24 10 D1
Basing View. RG21 3 D1
Baynard Clo. RG21 6 B6
Beachpiece Way. RG22 11 F4
Beaconsfield Rd. RG21 3 B5
Bear Ct. RG24 7 E6
Beaulieu Rd. RG21 10 C2
Beckett Clo. RG21 4 C6
Bedford Walk. RG21 3 B3
Beech Way. RG23 4 D3
Beecham Berry. RG22 11 F5
Beechwood Clo. RG22 11 F5
Beethoven Rd. RG22 9 F5
Beggarwood La. RG22 11 E6
Begonia Clo. RG22 8 B5
Bell Rd. RG24 6 D6
Belle Vue Rd. RG24 11 G1
Belmont Heights. RG22 11 G6
Belvedere Gdns. RG24 7 F1
Bennet Clo. RG21 6 C6
Berewyk Clo. RG24 11 E4
Berkeley Dri. RG22 9 G5
Bermuda Clo. RG24 6 B3
Bernstein Rd. RG22 8 D5
Berwyn Clo. RG22 8 C2
Bessemer Rd. RG21 9 G3
Beverley Clo. RG22 10 A6
Bexmoor Way. RG24 7 F6
Bilton Rd. RG24 6 D4
Binfields Clo. RG24 7 E4
Birches Crest. RG22 11 G5
Birchwood. RG24 7 E1
Bittern Clo. RG22 8 B5
Black Dam Way. RG21 10 C3
Blackberry Walk. RG24 7 E5
Blackbird Clo. RG22 8 A5
Blackdown Clo. RG22 8 C2
Blackthorn Way. RG23 4 D4
Blackwater Clo. RG21 10 C2
Blair Rd. RG21 3 A5
Blenheim Rd. RG24 11 G2
Bliss Clo. RG22 9 F3
Blunden Clo. RG21 9 G3
Bolton Cres. RG22 9 F1
Bond Clo. RG24 6 D4
Borodin Clo. RG22 9 G4
Bounty Rise. RG21 3 A5
Bounty Road. RG21 3 A5
Bourne Ct. RG22 10 C2
Bowman Rd. RG24 7 E1
Bowyer Clo. RG21 5 H5
Boyce Clo. RG24 8 D4
Bracken Bank. RG24 7 E5
Brackley Way. RG22 8 D3
Brahms Clo. RG22 9 F5
Brahms Rd. RG22 9 F5
Braine l'Alleud Rd. RG21 3 C1
Bramble Way. RG24 11 H1
Bramblys Clo. RG21 3 A4
Bramblys Dri. RG21 3 A4
Brambling Clo. RG22 8 B5
Bramdown Heights. RG22 11 F5
Brampton Gdns. RG22 11 H1
Branton Clo. RG22 8 D1
Brewer Clo. RG22 8 D1
Brickfields Clo. RG24 7 E5
Brighton Way. RG22 9 E4
Britten Rd. RG22 9 F5
Broadhurst Gro. RG24 7 E6
Brocas Dri. RG21 6 B6

Brookfield Clo. RG24 7 F1
Brookvale Clo. RG21 5 H5
Browning Clo. RG24 6 B5
Brunel Rd. RG21 5 F4
Brunswick Pl. RG22 9 G3
Buckby La. RG21 10 C2
Buckfast Clo. RG24 5 H2
Buckingham Par. RG22 8 B4
Buckland Av. RG22 9 E3
Buckskin La. RG22 8 B3
Budds Clo. RG21 5 H6
Bunnian Pl. RG21 3 C1
Bunting Mews. RG22 8 B6
Burgess Rd. RG21 10 A1
Burnaby Clo. RG22 8 D1
Burns Clo. RG24 6 B4
Burrow Flds. RG22 11 F6
Bury Rd. RG23 5 E4
Burtons Gdns. RG24 7 F6
Butler Clo. RG22 8 D1
Buttermere Dri. RG22 8 C4
Byfleet Av. RG24 11 G1
Byrd Gdns. RG24 8 D5
Byron Clo. RG24 6 B4

Caernarvon Clo. RG23 4 D5
Caesar Clo. RG23 4 D3
Cairngorm Clo. RG22 8 D1
Calleva Clo. RG22 11 F4
Cam Walk. RG21 10 C2
Camberry Clo. RG21 3 D6
Cambrian Way. RG22 8 C2
Camfield Clo. RG21 10 B4
Camlea Clo. RG21 10 B4
Campsie Clo. RG22 8 C1
Camrose Way. RG21 3 D6
Camwood Clo. RG21 10 B4
Canterbury Clo. RG22 8 C5
Carbonel Clo. RG23 4 C6
Carisbrooke Clo. RG23 4 D4
Carlisle Clo. RG23 4 D4
Carmichael Way. RG22 8 D5
Carpenters Down. RG24 6 B3
Castle Rd. RG21 3 C5
Castle Sq. RG21 3 B1
Castons Walk. RG21 3 C4
Castons Yard. RG21 3 B4
Catkin Clo. RG24 7 E2
Cavalier Clo. RG24 11 G1
Cavalier Rd. RG24 11 G1
Cavel Ct. RG24 7 F4
Cayman Clo. RG24 6 C4
Cedar Way. RG23 5 E4
Centre Dri. RG24 7 F4
Centurion Way. RG22 11 F4
Chaffinch Clo. RG22 8 B4
Chalk Vale. RG24 11 H2
Challis Clo. RG22 8 D3
Challoner Clo. RG22 9 E2
Chandler Rd. RG21 9 H3
Chantry Mews. RG21 11 F4
Chapel Hill. RG21 3 A1
Charldon Grn. RG24 7 F4
Charles Richards Clo.
RG21 3 A6
Charles St. RG21 9 F1
Charnwood Clo. RG22 8 C1
Chatworth Grn. RG22 11 G5
Chaucer Clo. RG24 6 B4
Chelmer Ct. RG21 10 C2
Chequers Rd. RG21 3 C3
Chester Pl. RG21 5 H6
Chesterfield Rd. RG21 3 D6
Chestnut Bank. RG22 7 G6
Cheviot Clo. RG22 8 D1
Chichester Pl. RG22 9 F3
Chiltern Ridge. RG21 11 F6
Chiltern Rd. RG22 8 C2
Chiltern Way. RG22 8 C2
Chineham La,
Popley Way. RG24 6 A3
Chineham La,
Shakespeare Rd. RG24 6 C5
Chineham Park Ct. RG24 6 C4
Chivers Clo. RG22 8 D2
Chopin Rd. RG22 9 E4
Church La,
Basingstoke. RG21 3 B3
Church La,
Cliddesden. RG25 9 H6
Church La,
Old Basing. RG24 7 F6
Church La,
Worting. RG23 4 B6
Church Sq. RG21 3 B3
Church St. RG21 3 B2
Churchill Way. RG21 3 A2

Churchill Way E. RG21 3 D2
Churchill Way W. RG21 3 A2
Churn Clo. RG22 7 G6
Cibbons Rd. RG24 7 E2
Claudius Dri. RG23 4 D3
Claythorpe Rd. RG22 8 D2
Cleaver Rd. RG22 8 D2
Clere Gdns. RG24 7 E3
Cleveland Clo. RG22 8 C2
Cliddesden Ct. RG21 10 A4
Cliddesden La. RG21 11 F6
Cliddesden Rd. RG21 3 C6
Clifton Ter. RG21 3 C1
Clifton Walk. RG21 3 B2
Clover Field. RG24 7 E5
Coates Clo. RG22 9 G3
Cobbett Grn. RG22 9 F2
Coffelle Clo. RG24 7 F2
Coleman Clo. RG21 6 B5
College Rd. RG21 5 G5
Colne Way. RG21 10 C2
Columbine Rd. RG22 8 B5
Colyer Clo. RG22 8 B5
Coniston Rd. RG22 8 C4
Constable Clo. RG21 10 C4
Constantine Way. RG22 11 E5
Coombehurst Dri. RG21 10 A5
Copland Clo. RG22 8 D5
Coppice Mews. RG23 4 D4
Copse Fields. RG24 7 F4
Copse View Clo. RG24 7 E1
Cordale Rd. RG21 3 A5
Corelli Rd. RG22 9 G5
Corfe Walk. RG23 5 E4
Corinthian Clo. RG22 11 F4
Cormorant Clo. RG22 8 B5
Cornish Clo. RG22 8 D2
Coronation Rd. RG21 10 B1
Cotswold Clo. RG21 8 C1
Cottle Clo. RG21 9 H3
Council Rd. RG21 3 B5
Coventry Rd. RG22 8 C5
Cowdrey Clo. RG21 6 B5
Cowslip Bank. RG24 7 E5
Crabtree Way. RG24 11 F2
Cranbourne Clo. RG21 9 G3
Cranbourne La. RG21 9 G3
Crockford La. RG24 6 D2
Crofters Meadow. RG24 7 E5
Cromwell Clo. RG21 11 G1
Cromwell Rd. RG21 10 A1
Cropmark Way. RG22 11 F4
Cross St. RG21 3 B3
Crossborough Gdns.
RG21 3 D3
Crossborough Hill.
RG21 3 D3
Crown La. RG24 11 F1
Cuddesden Ct. RG21 10 A4
Culver Rd. RG21 3 A6
Cumberland Av. RG22 9 F4
Curlew Clo. RG22 8 B5
Cyprus Rd. RG22 11 G6

Daffodil Clo. RG22 8 C5
Dahlia Clo. RG22 8 C5
Dalewood. RG22 8 C2
Damsel Path. RG21 10 C2
Danebury Rd. RG22 11 F5
Daneshill Dri. RG24 7 E4
Dankworth Rd. RG22 10 E5
Darent Cl. RG21 10 C2
Darlington Rd. RG21 6 A6
Dartmouth Walk. RG22 9 E2
Dartmouth Way. RG22 8 D2
Davy Clo. RG21 5 F6
Deanes Clo. RG21 10 B1
Deep La. RG21 5 G5
Delibes Clo. RG22 9 G5
Delius Clo. RG22 9 F4
Denham Dri. RG22 8 D3
Dewpond Walk. RG21 7 E5
Devonshire Clo. RG21 9 H1
Diana Clo. RG22 9 F2
Dibley Clo. RG22 8 D3
Dickens La. RG24 11 E5
Dominica Clo. RG24 6 B3
Domitian Gdns. RG24 4 D2
Dorchester Clo. RG23 4 D3
Dorrel Clo. RG22 11 F5
Doswell Way. RG21 10 B1
Dove Clo. RG22 8 B3
Dover Clo. RG23 5 E5
Downsland Rd. RG21 3 A4
Dragonfly Dri. RG24 7 E5
Dryden Clo. RG24 6 B4

Duddon Way. RG21 10 C2
Dudley Clo. RG23 4 D5
Dunsford Cres. RG23 4 D4
Durham Way. RG22 8 D5

Eagle Clo. RG22 8 B5
Eagle Ct. RG24 7 E6
Eastfield Av. RG21 3 D2
Eastrop La. RG21 3 D2
Eastrop Way. RG21 3 D2
Edgehill Clo. RG22 8 D1
Edison Rd. RG21 5 F3
Elbow Cnr. RG21 3 B2
Elderberry Bank. RG24 7 E5
Elgar Clo. RG22 9 F4
Elizabeth Rd. RG22 9 F1
Ellington Dri. RG22 9 E6
Elmwood Way. RG23 4 D4
Ennerdale Clo. RG22 8 C3
Esher Clo. RG22 9 E3
Essex Rd. RG21 3 A3
Eton Clo. RG22 11 E5
Euskirchen Way. RG23 5 E5
Exeter Clo. RG22 8 D5

Fabian Clo. RG21 5 H6
Fairfields Ct. RG21 3 C5
Fairfields Rd. RG21 3 C5
Fairthorne Rise. RG24 11 H1
Falcon Clo. RG22 8 B4
Falkland Rd. RG24 6 B3
Faraday Rd. RG24 6 C5
Farleigh Rise. RG21 10 B5
Farleigh Road. RG25 9 G6
Farm View Dri. RG22 7 F1
Faroe Clo. RG24 6 C4
Fayrewood Chase.
RG22 11 F4
Feathers La. RG21 3 C3
Feathers Yd. RG21 3 C3
Feld Way. RG24 7 F5
Fencott Pl. RG21 10 A1
Fennel Clo. RG24 7 F1
Ferguson Clo. RG21 10 A5
Firecrest Rd. RG24 8 A6
Firs Way. RG23 4 D4
Fiske Clo. RG22 4 D6
Flaxfield Ct. RG21 3 A3
Flaxfield Rd. RG21 3 A3
Fletcher Clo. RG21 5 G6
Florence Way. RG24 4 D2
Forest Dri. RG24 7 E1
Fountains Clo. RG24 5 H1
Four Lanes Clo. RG24 7 F2
Foxglove Clo. RG22 8 B5
Fox's Furlong. RG24 7 E5
Foyle Park. RG21 10 A5
Frances Rd. RG21 3 A4
Fraser Clo. RG24 11 G1
Freemantle Clo. RG21 6 C5
Frescade Cres. RG21 3 A5
Frithmead Clo. RG21 9 H2
Frome Clo. RG21 10 C2
Fulmar Clo. RG22 8 A6
Fuzzy Drove. RG22 8 A5
Fylingdales Clo. RG22 8 C1

Gage Clo. RG24 7 E6
Gainsborough Rd.
RG21 10 C4
Galloway Clo. RG22 8 D2
Gander Dri. RG24 4 D2
Gannet Clo. RG22 8 A5
Gefferys Fields. RG21 3 D3
George St. RG21 5 G5
Gershwin Ct. RG22 9 E4
Gershwin Rd. RG22 8 D5
Gilbard Clo. RG21 5 F2
Gilbert Clo. RG24 6 B3
Gillies Dri. RG24 4 D2
Glade Clo. RG24 7 E3
Glastonbury Clo. RG24 5 H2
Glebe La. RG23 4 C6
Gloucester Dri. RG22 8 D5
Goat La. RG21 3 C2
Goldfinch Gdns. RG22 8 A6
Goodman Clo. RG21 5 G6
Gordon Clo. RG21 6 B6
Gower Clo. RG24 6 A6
Gracemere Cres. RG22 8 A5
Grafton Way. RG22 5 E6
Grainger Clo. RG24 9 F4
Grampian Way. RG22 8 C2
Great Binfields Cres.
RG24 7 E5
Great Binfields Rd. RG24 7 E3
Great Oaks Chase. RG24 6 D3

Grebe Clo. RG22 8 B5
Green Way. RG22 4 D5
Greenbirch Clo. RG22 8 B5
Greenbury Clo. RG24 4 D5
Greenwood Dri. RG24 7 E5
Gregory Clo. RG21 6 B6
Gresley Rd. RG21 10 B1
Greywell Rd. RG25 11 H2
Grieg Clo. RG22 9 F4
Grosvenor Clo. RG22 11 F6
Grove Clo. RG21 10 B4
Grove Rd. RG21 10 A5
Guernsey Clo. RG24 6 B2
Guinea Ct. RG24 7 F1

Hackwood Cotts. RG21 10 B4
Hackwood Rd. RG21 3 C5
Hadleigh Pl. RG21 3 A3
Hadrians Way. RG23 4 D3
Hailstone Rd. RG21 6 A5
Halliday Clo. RG21 9 G3
Hamble Clo. RG21 10 C2
Hamelyn Clo. RG21 9 H1
Hamelyn Rd. RG21 9 H1
Hamilton Clo. RG21 5 F3
Hammond Rd. RG21 3 A5
Hampshire Clo. RG22 8 C1
Handel Clo. RG22 9 F4
Hanmore Rd. RG24 6 D2
Hanover Gdns. RG21 9 H2
Hardy La. RG21 9 H1
Harlech Clo. RG23 4 D5
Harris Hill. RG22 11 E4
Hartswood. RG24 7 E3
Harvest Way. RG24 7 E5
Hastings Clo. RG23 4 D5
Hatch La. RG24 11 G1
Hatch Warren Gdns.
RG22 9 F5
Hatch Warren La,
Brighton Hill. RG22 9 F6
Hatch Warren La,
Kempshott. RG22 8 C5
Hathaway Gdns. RG24 6 C5
Hawk Clo. RG22 8 B4
Hawkfield La. RG21 3 A5
Hawthorn Way. RG23 4 D4
Haydn Rd. RG22 9 E5
Hazeldene. RG24 7 E2
Hazelwood Clo. RG23 5 E3
Hazelwood Dri. RG22 9 E5
Headington Clo. RG22 9 E5
Heather Way. RG22 8 B5
Heathfield Rd. RG22 9 E5
Hele Clo. RG21 9 H3
Hepplewhite Dri. RG22 11 E4
Hereford Rd. RG23 4 D5
Heritage Park. RG22 11 F6
Heritage Vw. RG22 11 F6
Heron Park. RG24 7 E4
Heron Way. RG22 8 B5
High Dri. RG22 9 E3
High Moors. RG22 7 E2
Highdowns. RG22 11 G5
Higher Mead. RG24 7 E5
Highfield Chase. RG22 5 G6
Highlands Rd. RG22 8 C1
Highwood Ridge. RG22 11 F5
Hill Sq. RG24 7 F4
Hill View Rd. RG22 9 F2
Hillary Rd. RG21 5 G4
Hillcrest Clo. RG23 4 D5
Hillcrest Walk. RG23 4 D5
Hogarth Clo. RG21 10 D3
Holbein Clo. RG21 10 C4
Hollins Walk. RG21 3 B2
Holly Dri. RG24 11 G1
Hollyhock Clo. RG22 8 C5
Holmes Clo. RG22 11 F5
Holst Clo. RG22 9 F5
Holy Barn Clo. RG22 8 B4
Homesteads Rd. RG22 8 B4
Honeysuckle Clo. RG24 7 E5
Hoppersmead. RG25 9 H6
Hopton Garth. RG24 7 F4
Houndmills Rd. RG21 5 F4
Howard Rd. RG21 10 B4
Hubbard Rd. RG21 5 G3
Huish La. RG24 11 G2
Hulbert Way. RG22 8 D3
Hutton Clo. RG24 6 B5
Hyacinth Clo. RG22 8 C5

INDUSTRIAL ESTATES:
Brighton Hills Retail Pk.
RG21 9 F3
Cartel Business Centre.
RG24 6 D5

Chineham Business Pk. RG24 6 D1
Daneshill East Ind Est. RG24 6 D6
Gastons Wood Ind Est. RG24 6 D4
Hampshire International Business Pk. RG24 6 D1
Houndmills Ind Est. RG21 5 G4
Intec Business Centre. RG24 6 D5
Kingsland Ind Park. RG24 6 D4
Moniton Trading Est. RG23 4 C6
Viables Ind Est. RG22 9 H4
West Ham Est. RG22 5 E6
Woodlands Business Village. RG24 6 C6
Inglewood Dri. RG22 11 F5
Inkpen Gdns. RG24 7 F5
Iris Clo. RG22 8 B5
Irwell Clo. RG21 10 C2
Ivar Gdns. RG24 7 F4

Jackdaw Clo. RG22 8 B5
Jacobs Alley. RG21 3 C4
Jacobs Yard. RG21 3 C4
James Clo. RG21 6 B5
Jasmine Clo. RG22 8 C5
Jays Clo. RG22 9 G4
Jefferson Rd. RG21 6 B5
Jersey Clo. RG24 6 B2
Joices Yard. RG21 3 B3
Joule Par. RG21 5 G4
Jubilee Rd. RG21 3 B4
Julius Clo. RG24 4 D2
June Dri. RG23 4 C5
Juniper Clo. RG24 7 F1

Kathleen Clo. RG21 9 H3
Keats Clo. RG24 6 C4
Kelvin Hill. RG22 9 F2
Kempshott Gdns. RG22 8 B5
Kempshott Gro. RG22 8 C1
Kempshott La. RG22 8 B6
Kendal Gdns. RG22 8 C3
Kenilworth Rd. RG23 4 D4
Kennet Clo. RG21 10 C2
Kestrel Rd. RG22 8 B4
Ketelby Rise. RG22 9 G5
Kimball Rd. RG21 9 G2
Kimber Clo. RG24 7 E2
Kimberley Rd. RG22 9 F2
Kingfisher Clo. RG22 8 B4
Kings Furlong Dri. RG21 9 G1
Kings Pightle. RG24 7 E2
Kings Rd. RG22 9 F1
Kingsclere Rd, Houndmills. RG21 5 G3
Kingsclere Rd. RG23 5.E3
Kingsmill Rd. RG21 9 H3
Kipling Walk. RG22 9 F2
Knight St. RG21 5 G6

Laburnum Way. RG23 5 E4
Lambs Row. RG24 7 E6
Lancaster Rd. RG21 5 H4
Landseer Clo. RG21 10 C4
Lansley Rd. RG21 6 A5
Lapin La. RG22 11 F6
Larchwood. RG24 7 E1
Lark Clo. RG22 8 B4
Larkfield. RG24 7 E2
Lavender Rd. RG22 8 C5
Lawrence Clo. RG24 6 B4
Lea Clo. RG21 10 C2
Lefroy Av. RG21 6 B6
Lehar Clo. RG22 9 E4
Lennon Way. RG22 8 D5
Lennox Rd. RG22 9 F3
Lewis Clo. RG21 6 C6
Lightfoot Gro. RG21 10 A5
Lilac Way. RG23 5 E4
Lily Clo. RG22 8 B5
Lime Gdns. RG21 10 D2
Lime Tree Way. RG24 6 D2
Lincoln Clo. RG22 8 D5
Linden Av. RG24 11 F2
Lingfield Clo. RG22 11 H2
Linnet Clo. RG22 8 B3
Lion Ct. RG22 7 E6
Lister Rd. RG22 9 G2
Little Basing. RG24 7 E5
Little Copse Chase. RG24 6 D2

Little Fallow. RG24 7 F5
*Locksmead, New Bridge La. RG21 10 D2
Loddon Dri. RG21 10 C2
Loddon Mall. RG21 3 B2
Loggon Rd. RG21 9 H3
London Rd, Basingstoke. RG21 3 C4
London Rd, Old Basing. RG24 11 E2
London St. RG21 3 C4
Long Copse Chase. RG24 6 D2
Long Cross La. RG22 11 E5
Long La. RG24 7 F3
Longacre Rise. RG24 6 D3
Longcroft Clo. RG21 5 H6
Longfellow Par. RG24 6 B5
Longmoor Rd. RG21 9 H1
Longstock Clo. RG24 7 G1
Love Groves. RG24 7 F2
Loveridge Clo. RG21 9 H3
Lower Brook St. RG21 5 G5
Lower Chestnut Dri. RG21 9 G2
Lower Wote St. RG21 3 C2
Lowland Rd. RG22 8 B5
Loyalty La. RG24 11 G1
Ludlow Clo. RG23 5 E5
Ludlow Gdns. RG23 5 E5
Lundy Clo. RG24 6 C4
Lune Clo. RG21 10 C2
Lupin Clo. RG22 8 B5
Lutyens Clo. RG24 7 E4
Lyford Rd. RG21 10 B1
Lymington Clo. RG22 11 F5
Lyn Ct. RG21 10 C2
Lyndhurst Dri. RG22 11 G5
Lytton Rd. RG21 10 B2

Madeira Clo. RG24 6 C3
Magnolia Ct. RG24 5 H1
Magnus Dri. RG22 11 F4
Majestic Clo. RG22 11 E6
Mahler Clo. RG22 9 G5
Maldive Rd. RG24 6 C3
Malham Gdns. RG22 11 F6
Mallard Clo. RG22 8 A6
Malta Clo. RG24 6 B3
Malvern Clo. RG22 8 C2
Manor Clo. RG22 11E5
Manor La. RG24 7 G6
Mansfield Rd. RG22 9 F3
Mapie Clo. RG22 8 B5
Maple Cres. RG21 6 A5
Maplehurst Chase. RG22 11 F6
Margaret Rd. RG22 9 E1
Marigold Clo. RG24 8 C5
Market Pl. RG21 3 B3
Mark La. RG21 3 C4
Marlowe Clo. RG24 6 B5
Marshall Gdns. RG21 6 B6
Marshcourt. RG24 7 E5
Martin Clo. RG21 6 C5
Martins Wood. RG24 7 E2
Mathias Walk. RG22 9 E6
Matilda Dri. RG22 11 F4
Mattock Way. RG24 6 D2
Maw Clo. RG24 9 G5
May Clo. RG24 11 H1
May Pl. RG21 3 C3
May St. RG21 5 G5
Maybrook. RG24 7 E1
Mayfield Ridge. RG24 11 F6
Mayflower Clo. RG24 6 D2
Maynards Wood. RG24 6 D2
McCartney Walk. RG22 8 D5
Meadow Ridge. RG22 11 G6
Meadow Rd. RG21 9 H3
Meadowland. RG24 6 D2
Medway Ct. RG21 10 C2
Melford Gdns. RG22 8 B2
Melrose Walk. RG24 5 G2
Mendip Clo. RG22 8 C2
Meon Walk. RG21 10 C2
Mercer Clo. RG22 4 D6
Merlin Mead. RG22 8 B6
Merriat Clo. RG21 10 A5
Merrileas Gdns. RG22 8 C4
Merrydown La. RG24 7 E1
Merryfield. RG24 6 D2
Merton Rd. RG21 6 C5
Middleton Gdns. RG21 10 D6
Midlane Clo. RG21 9 H3
Milkingpen La. RG24 7 G6
Mill Rd. RG24 4 D2

Milton Clo. RG24 6 C4
Minden Clo. RG24 6 D3
Mitchell Gdns. RG22 8 D5
Monarch Clo. RG22 11 E6
Mongers Piece. RG24 7 F1
Montague Pl. RG21 3 C5
Montserrat Clo. RG24 6 B3
Montserrat Clo. RG24 6 B3
Moor View. RG24 7 F6
Moorfoot Gdns. RG22 8 D2
Moorhams Av. RG22 11 E5
Morley Rd. RG21 9 H3
Morse Rd. RG22 5 F6
Mortimer La. RG21 3 A3
Mourne Clo. RG22 8 C1
Mozart Clo. RG22 9 F5
Mulberry Way. RG22 7 E1
Mullins Clo. RG21 6 B5
Munnings Clo. RG21 10 C4
Musgrave Clo. RG22 9 E5
Musket Copse. RG24 10 F1
Myland Clo. RG24 6 B5

Napoleon Dri. RG23 5 E3
Nash Clo. RG21 6 B6
Neath Rd. RG21 10 C2
Neville Clo. RG21 10 A5
New Bridge La. RG21 10 D2
New Market Sq. RG21 3 C2
New Rd. RG21 3 B4
New St. RG21 3 B3
Nightingale Gdns. RG24 4 D2
Norden Clo. RG21 10 A1
Normanton Rd. RG21 6 A5
Norn Hill. RG21 6 B6
Norn Hill Clo. RG21 6 B6
Northgate Way. RG21 11 E5
Norton Ride. RG24 7 E6
Norwich Clo. RG22 8 D5
Norwood Gdns. RG21 9 G3
Nuffield Clo. RG24 9 E6
Nursery Clo. RG24 7 E2

Oak Clo. RG21 10 D2
Oaklands Way. RG23 4 D4
Oakridge Rd. RG21 6 A5
Oakwood. RG24 7 E1
Ochil Clo. RG22 8 C2
Octavian Clo. RG22 11 F4
Old Basing Mall. RG21 3 B2
Old Canal Pl. RG21 10 C2
Old Common Rd. RG21 10 C3
Old Down Clo. RG22 8 B4
Old Kempshott La. RG22 8 B2
Old Reading Rd. RG21 3 D1
Old Worting Rd. RG22 4 D6
Oldberg Gdns. RG22 9 G5
Olivers Walk. RG24 7 E6
Onslow Clo. RG24 6 D4
Orchard Rd. RG22 8 D1
Orkney Clo. RG24 6 C4
Osbourne Clo. RG21 5 G3
Osprey Rd. RG22 8 B4
Oyster Clo. RG21 11 E5

Pack La. RG22 8 A2
Packenham Rd. RG21 9 G1
Paddock Rd. RG22 9 E2
Paddockfields. RG24 7 G5
Pages Bungalows. RG21 3 A3
Palmer Clo. RG21 6 B5
Park Av. RG24 11 F2
Park Gdns. RG21 10 C4
Park La. RG21 11 F2
Parkside Rd. RG21 3 D6
Parkwood Clo. RG24 7 E1
Paterson Clo. RG22 8 D5
Paulet Pl. RG21 11 G1
Paxton Clo. RG21 11 E4
Peake Clo. RG24 7 E6
Pelham Clo. RG24 11 G2
Pelton Rd. RG21 5 G4
Pembroke Rd. RG23 4 D5
Pemerton Rd. RG21 6 B5
Pendennis Clo. RG23 4 D4
Pennine Clo. RG22 8 C2
Pennine Way. RG22 8 C2
Penrith Rd. RG21 3 A4
Pentland Clo. RG22 8 C1
Pershore Rd. RG24 6 A4
Petersfield Clo. RG21 7 F1
Petrel Croft. RG22 8 B5
Pettys Brook Rd. RG24 7 E1
Petunia Clo. RG22 8 B5
Petworth Clo. RG22 11 F5
Peveral Walk. RG22 9 E1

Peveral Way. RG22 9 E2
Pheasant Clo. RG22 8 A4
Pheby Rd. RG22 9 E3
Phoenix Park Ter. RG21 10 A1
Pimpernel Way. RG24 7 E5
Pinkerton Rd. RG22 8 D2
Pinnell Clo. RG22 11 E5
Pintail Clo. RG22 8 B6
Pitcairn Clo. RG24 6 C3
Pitman Clo. RG22 8 D3
Pittard Rd. RG21 9 G1
Plover Clo. RG22 8 B3
Popley Way. RG24 5 G2
Poppy Fields. RG24 7 F5
Porchester Sq. RG21 3 B2
Portacre Rise. RG21 9 G1
Porter Rd. RG22 9 G4
Portsmouth Cres. RG22 9 E2
Portsmouth Walk. RG22 9 E3
Portsmouth Walk. RG22 9 E2
Portway. RG23 4 C5
Potters Walk. RG21 3 B3
Poynings Clo. RG21 10 B5
Priestley Rd. RG24 7 E3
Primrose Gdns. RG22 11 F6
Princes Cres. RG22 9 F2
Priory Gdns. RG21 7 G6
Privett Clo. RG24 7 F4
Puffin Clo. RG22 8 B6
Purcell Clo. RG22 9 G4
Puttenham Rd. RG24 7 F2
Pyotts Copse. RG24 7 F4
Pyotts Ct. RG24 7 F3
Pyotts Hill. RG24 7 F3

Queen Annes Wk. RG21 3 C3
Queen Mary Av. RG21 3 A6
Queens Rd. RG21 5 G5
Queensdale Ct. RG21 9 H1
Quilter Rd. RG22 8 D4

Radford Gdns. RG21 9 G3
Radwick Clo. RG21 9 H3
Rainbow Clo. RG24 11 H2
Rainham Clo. RG22 8 B6
Rankine Rd. RG24 6 C5
Raphael Clo. RG22 9 G4
Ravel Clo. RG22 9 F4
Rayleigh Rd. RG21 3 A2
Reading Rd. RG24 6 C5
Red Lion La. RG21 3 C3
Redbridge La. RG24 10 D2
Redwing Rd. RG22 8 B6
Remembrance Gdns. RG24 6 D3
Rembrandt Clo. RG21 10 C4
Renoir Clo. RG21 10 C4
Renown Way. RG24 7 E1
Restormel Clo. RG23 4 D4
Reynolds Clo. RG21 10 C2
Ribble Way. RG21 10 C2
Richmond Rd. RG22 8 D5
Ridge Clo. RG22 11 G6
Riley La. RG24 7 G6
Ringway East. RG21 10 D1
Ringway North. RG21 5 F3
Ringway South. RG21 3 A6
Ringway West. RG21 5 F3
Riverside Clo. RG24 7 G5
Robin Clo. RG22 8 B4
Roding Clo. RG21 10 C2
Rochester Clo. RG22 8 D5
Rochford Rd. RG21 5 H5
Roentgen Rd. RG24 7 E6
Roman Rd. RG23 4 C6
Roman Way. RG23 5 H2
Romsey Clo. RG24 7 G5
Rooksdown Av. RG24 4 D2
Rooksdown La. RG24 4 D2
Rose Clo. RG24 8 C5
Rose Hodson Pl. RG23 4 D3
Roseberry Clo. RG24 8 C6
Rosehip Way. RG24 7 E5
Ross Clo. RG21 9 H3
Rossini Clo. RG22 9 F5
Rothay Ct. RG21 10 C2
Roundmead Clo. RG21 9 H3
Royal Clo. RG22 11 E6
Rubens Clo. RG21 10 C4
Ruskin Clo. RG21 10 D4
Russell Rd. RG21 3 C6
Rutherford Rd. RG24 6 C5
Rydal Clo. RG22 8 C3

St Davids Rd. RG22 9 F2
St Gabriels Lea. RG24 7 F4
St Johns Walk. RG21 3 B2
St Leonards Av. RG24 7 F2
St Marys Ct. RG21 3 D2
St Michaels Rd. RG25 5 D2
St Patricks Rd. RG22 9 F2
St Pauls Rd. RG22 9 F1
St Peters Rd. RG22 8 D1
St Thomas Clo. RG21 5 H4
Salisbury Gdns. RG22 9 E1
Sandbanks Dri. RG22 11 F4
Sandpiper Way. RG22 8 A5
Sandringham Ct. RG22 9 F1
Sandys Clo. RG22 9 F1
Sandys Rd. RG22 9 F1
Sarum Hill. RG21 3 A3
Saxon Way. RG24 7 E6
Scharlatti Rd. RG22 9 G5
Schroeder Clo. RG22 9 H2
Schubert Rd. RG22 9 F5
Scotney Rd. RG21 6 A5
Seagull Clo. RG22 8 B5
Seal Rd. RG21 3 C3
Selby Walk. RG24 6 A4
Severn Way. RG21 10 C2
Seymour Rd. RG22 8 D3
Shakespeare Rd. RG24 6 B4
Shelley Clo. RG24 6 C5
Sheppard Rd. RG21 9 G3
Sheraton Av. RG22 11 F4
Sherborne Rd. RG21 5 H3
Sherrington Way. RG22 9 G3
Sherwood Clo. RG22 11 G5
Shetland Rd. RG24 6 B3
Shipton Way. RG22 8 D3
Shooters Way. RG21 6 B6
Sibelius Clo. RG22 9 F5
Sidlaw Clo. RG22 8 C2
Silvester Clo. RG21 6 C6
Simmons Walk. RG21 10 C2
Simons Clo. RG24 7 E3
Simons Rd. RG24 6 D3
Skippets Lane E. RG21 10 B5
Skippets Lane W. RG21 10 B5
Snowdrop Clo. RG22 9 G5
Solbys Rd. RG21 5 H5
Solent Dri. RG22 11 F4
Sonning Clo. RG22 8 B6
Soper Gro. RG21 10 A1
Sorrells Clo. RG24 7 E2
South Ham Rd. RG22 9 F1
Southend Rd. RG21 3 A2
Southern Rd. RG21 3 B4
Southlands. RG24 6 D2
Speckled Wood Rd. RG24 6 A3
Sperrin Clo. RG22 8 C2
Stag Hill. RG22 9 E2
Stag Oak La. RG24 6 D1
Stanford Rd. RG24 6 B5
Starling Clo. RG22 8 B4
Station App. RG21 3 B1
Station Mall. RG21 3 B1
Station Rd. RG25 9 H6
Stephenson Rd. RG21 5 F4
Stewart Rd. RG24 6 D4
Stockbridge Clo. RG24 7 F1
Stocker Clo. RG21 10 A5
Stratfield Rd. RG21 6 A5
Stratton Rd. RG21 9 G3
Strauss Rd. RG22 9 G5
Stravinsky Rd. RG22 9 G5
Stroud Clo. RG22 6 D3
Stroudley Rd. RG24 6 D5
Stubbs Rd. RG21 10 C5
Stukeley Rd. RG21 5 G6
Sullivan Rd. RG22 9 F4
Summerfield. RG24 7 F1
Sunflower Clo. RG22 8 C5
Sutton Rd. RG21 6 A6
Swallow Clo. RG22 8 B4
Swing Swang La. RG24 6 D5
Sycamore Way. RG23 5 E3
Sylvia Clo. RG21 3 A5

Tallis Gdns. RG22 9 F4
Talmey Clo. RG24 6 C4
Tamarisk Clo. RG22 11 G6
Tangway. RG24 7 E1
Tasmania Clo. RG24 6 B3
Taverner Clo. RG21 6 C6
Teal Cres. RG22 8 A5
Telford Rd. RG21 5 F4
Tennyson Way. RG22 9 F2
Ternns Clo. RG21 8 B6
Test Way. RG22 10 C2

Tewkesbury Clo. RG24 6 A4
Thames Ct. RG21 10 C2
The Beeches. RG22 11 G5
The Brackens. RG22 11 G5
*The Butty,
 The Moorings. RG21 10 C2
The Cornfields. RG22 11 G4
The Croft. RG22 11 G5
The Danes. RG21 3 C2
The Dell. RG25 11 H2
The Glebe. RG21 3 B2
The Harrow Way. RG22 9 F3
The Hedgerows. RG24 7 F4
The Laurels. RG21 6 C6
The Limes. RG24 8 B4
The Mead. RG24 11 G1
The Meadow. RG22 11 G6
The Moorings. RG21 10 C2
The Rushes. RG21 10 C2
The Street. RG24 7 F6
The Topiary. RG24 7 F4
The Wolds. RG22 8 D2
The Woodlands. RG24 7 F1
Thornhill Way. RG24 7 F1
Thrush Clo. RG22 8 B4
Thumwood. RG24 7 E2
Thyme Clo. RG24 7 E1
Tiberius Clo. RG23 4 D3
Timberlake Rd. RG21 3 A2
Timor Clo. RG24 6 B3
Tintagel Clo. RG23 4 D4
Tintern Clo. RG24 5 G2
Tippet Gdns. RG22 9 G5
Tiverton Rd. RG23 4 C6
Tobago Clo. RG24 6 A3
Tollway. RG24 7 F1
Townsend Clo. RG21 5 G6
Trellis Dri. RG22 7 F4
Trent Way. RG21 10 C2
Trinidad Clo. RG24 6 A4
Tulip Clo. RG22 8 C5
Turner Clo. RG21 10 D3
Tweedsmuir Rd. RG22 8 D1

Upfallow. RG24 7 F5
Upper Chestnut Dri.
 RG21 9 G2
Upper Sherborne Rd.
 RG21 5 G3
Upronfield Clo. RG22 11 F4
Upton Cres. RG21 5 H3

Van Dyck Clo. RG21 10 D3
Vanburgh Gdns. RG21 11 F4
Verdi Clo. RG22 9 E5
Veronica Clo. RG22 8 C5
Vespasian Gdns. RG24 4 D3
Viables La. RG22 10 A5
Victoria Pl. RG22 4 C6
Victoria St. RG21 3 B4
Violet Clo. RG22 8 B6
Vitellius Gdns. RG24 4 D2
Vivian Rd. RG21 6 B6
Vyne Rd. RG21 3 B1

Wade Rd. RG24 6 D4
Wagner Clo. RG22 9 F5
Wallins Copse. RG24 7 E3
Wallis Ct. RG23 5 E4
Wallis Rd. RG21 3 B5
Wallop Dri. RG21 11 E5
Warbleton Rd. RG24 7 F2
Warren Way. RG22 9 E1
Warton Rd. RG21 10 B1
Warwick Rd. RG23 4 D5
Water Way. RG21 10 C2
Wateridge Rd. RG21 6 B5
Waterlily Clo. RG21 10 C2
Waterloo Av. RG23 4 D3
Watling End. RG22 11 F4
Watson Way. RG23 5 E4
Wavell Clo. RG22 9 F2
Waverley Av. RG21 9 H2
Wayside Rd. RG24 4 C5
Weale Ct. RG21 10 A1
Webb Clo. RG24 7 E2
Wella Path. RG21 9 G2
Wella Rd. RG21 9 G2
Wellington Ter. RG23 4 D3
Welton Ct. RG21 5 H5
Wesley Walk. RG21 3 B2
Wessex Clo. RG21 9 H1
West Ham Clo. RG21 5 E6
West Ham La,
 Worting RG23 4 C6
West Ham La,
 Grafton Way. RG23 5 E6

Westbrook Ct. RG23 4 C6
Western Way. RG22 9 F1
Westfield Rd. RG21 3 D6
Westgate Clo. RG23 4 C5
Westminster Clo. RG22 8 C5
Westray Clo. RG21 6 C6
Westside Clo. RG22 9 E2
Weysprings Clo. RG21 10 C2
Whistler Clo. RG21 10 C4
White Hart La. RG21 3 D4
Whitehead Clo. RG24 7 E6
Whitestones. RG22 11 G5
Whitewood. RG24 7 E2
Whitney Rd. RG24 6 D6
Wicklow Ct. RG23 8 C1
Widmore Rd. RG22 8 D3
Wights Walk. RG22 11 F4
Willoughby Way. RG23 5 E4
Willow Way. RG23 5 E3
Wilmot Way. RG23 5 E4
Wilton Pl. RG21 5 G6
Winchcombe Rd. RG21 5 H6
Winchester Rd,
 Basingstoke. RG21 3 A5
Winchester Rd,
 Kempshott. RG22 8 B6
Winchester St. RG21 3 B4
Windermere Av. RG22 8 D3
Windrush Clo. RG21 10 C2
Windsor Gdns. RG21 11 E5
Winklebury Way. RG23 4 C5
Winterthur Way. RG21 3 A1
Winton Sq. RG21 3 B4
Woburn Gdns. RG22 9 E5
Wood Clo. RG22 11 F5
Woodbury Rd. RG21 11 F4
Woodgarston Dri. RG22 11 E5
Woodmere Croft. RG22 8 B6
Woodpecker Clo. RG22 8 A5
Woodroffe Dri. RG22 8 D3
Woods La. RG25 9 F6
Woodside Gdns. RG24 7 E2
Woodstock Mead. RG22 11 F6
Woodville La. RG24 7 E2
Woolford Way. RG23 5 E5
Worcester Av. RG23 8 C5
Wordsworth Clo. RG24 6 B5
Worting Rd. RG21 3 A3
Wote St. RG21 3 C3
Wrekin Clo. RG21 8 C1
Wykeham Dri. RG23 4 C6

Yellowhammer Rd.
 RG22 8 A6
York Clo. RG22 8 D5

Zinnia Clo. RG22 8 B6

HEATH END/ TADLEY

Abbotswood Clo. RG26 13 E5
Adam Clo. RG26 12 C2
Almswood Rd. RG26 12 D2
Ambrose Rd. RG26 13 E3
Appleshaw Clo. RG26 13 E4
Arnwood Av. RG26 13 G3
Ash La. RG26 12 B3
Ashurst Clo. RG26 12 D4
Barlows Rd. RG26 13 E4
Baughurst Rd. RG26 12 B3
Beavers Clo. RG26 12 D3
Binley Ct. RG26 13 F3
Birch Rd. RG26 12 C2
Bishops Clo. RG26 12 D2
Bishopswood La. RG26 12 B3
Bishopswood Rd. RG26 12 C3
Blakes La. RG26 13 E3
Bordon Clo. RG26 12 D4
Bowmonts Rd. RG26 13 F4
Bramblewood Dri. RG26 12 D2
Bramdean Clo. RG26 13 E4
Brampton Mdw. RG26 13 G4
Briar Way. RG26 13 F3
Brimpton Rd. RG26 12 A2
Broadhalfpenny La.
 RG26 13 F2
Broadoak. RG26 13 G3
Brook Grn. RG26 13 F4
Brookside Walk. RG26 13 F4
Burney Bit. RG26 12 C2
Burnham Rd. RG26 12 C2
Burnley Clo. RG26 13 E4
Candover Clo. RG26 13 E4

Carrington Cres. RG26 13 E3
Cedar Clo. RG26 13 G5
Cheriton Clo. RG26 13 E4
Chippendale Clo. RG26 12 B2
Christy Ct. RG26 13 E4
Church Brook. RG26 12 D5
Church Rd,
 Pamber Heath. RG26 13 G2
Church Rd,
 Tadley. RG26 13 E5
Churchill Clo. RG26 13 G5
Clapps Gate Rd. RG26 13 H2
Conifer Clo. RG26 12 B2
Coppice Clo. RG26 12 B3
Crookham Clo. RG26 13 E5
Deanswood Rd. RG26 12 D3
Denmead. RG26 13 E4
Douro Clo. RG26 12 B3
Droxford Cres. RG26 12 D4
Eastlyn Rd. RG26 13 H3
Elmhurst. RG26 13 E4
Erskine Clo. RG26 13 H2
Fairlawn Rd. RG26 13 F5
Fairoak Way. RG26 12 B2
Falcon Fields. RG26 13 E2
Farringdon Way. RG26 13 E4
Finch Clo. RG26 13 F4
Forest Clo. RG26 12 B2
Forest La. RG26 13 G5
Franklin Av. RG26 12 D2
Fullerton Way. RG26 13 F4
Furze Rd. RG26 12 C2
Georgina Gdns. RG26 13 G3
Giles Ct. RG26 13 F4
Giles Rd. RG26 13 F3
Glebe Clo. RG26 13 E4
Glendale Rd. RG26 12 D3
Gorselands. RG26 13 E3
Gravelly Clo. RG26 13 E5
Greywell Clo. RG26 12 D3
Gutteridge La. RG26 12 D4
Hamble Dri. RG26 13 G3
Hanger Rd. RG26 12 C2
Harmsworth Rd. RG26 13 E3
Hartley Gdns. RG26 13 E5
Hartshill Rd. RG26 12 B2
Hawkley Dri. RG26 12 B2
Hazel Grn. RG26 12 A3
Heath Clo. RG26 12 B2
Heath End Rd. RG26 12 B3
Heath Rd. RG26 13 G3
Heather Dri. RG26 12 C2
Heathlands. RG26 12 B2
Heathrow Copse. RG26 12 A3
Hedge End. RG26 13 F5
Hepplewhite Clo. RG26 12 B2
Herriard Way. RG26 13 E4
Hicks Clo. RG26 12 B2
Hillcrest. RG26 13 E3
Hinton Clo. RG26 13 E4
Honeybottom Rd. RG26 13 E3
Huntsmoor Rd. RG26 12 C3
Hylton Ct. RG26 13 F3
Hythe Clo. RG26 13 E4
Ilex Clo. RG26 13 H2
Inspire La. RG26 13 H2
INDUSTRIAL ESTATES:
 Calleva Pk Ind Est.
 RG26 12 B1
Inhurst La. RG26 12 A3
Inhurst Way. RG26 12 C3
Jubilee Clo. RG26 13 G2
Knapp La. RG26 13 F4
Knollys Clo. RG26 13 H2
Lamdens Walk. RG26 13 E4
Linton Clo. RG26 13 E5
Long Gro. RG26 12 A2
Main Rd. RG26 13 F5
Malthouse La. RG26 13 F5
Manse La. RG26 13 F5
Maple Gro. RG26 13 E4
Mariners Clo. RG26 13 G6
Meon Clo. RG26 12 D2
Millers Rd. RG26 13 E3
Minstead Clo. RG26 13 E5
Monkswood Cres. RG26 13 E5
Mornington Clo. RG26 12 B3
Mortimer Gdns. RG26 13 F5
Mount Pleasant. RG26 12 D3
Mount Pleasant Dri.
 RG26 12 D3
Mulfords Hill. RG26 13 E2
New Church Rd. RG26 13 E4
New Rd. RG26 12 C4
Newtown. RG26 12 D3
Northview Rd. RG26 13 F5

O'Bee Gdns. RG26 12 C2
Oak Clo. RG26 12 A3
Oak Tree Clo. RG26 13 E3
Oakfield Rd. RG26 13 H2
Odette Gdns. RG26 13 E3
Otterbourne Cres.
 RG26 13 E5
Pamber Heath Rd.
 RG26 13 G4
Pelican Rd. RG26 13 G2
Pinehurst. RG26 13 E4
Pinewood Clo. RG26 12 A2
Pinks La. RG26 12 B2
Plantation Rd. RG26 12 C2
Pleasant Hill. RG26 13 E3
Poplar Clo. RG26 12 B3
Portiswood Clo. RG26 13 G3
Portway. RG26 12 B2
Purbrook Rd. RG26 12 D4
Ramsdell Clo. RG26 13 E4
Rectory Clo. RG26 13 F5
Reubens Cres. RG26 13 E3
Reynards Clo. RG26 13 E3
Rimes La. RG26 12 C5
Romans Gate. RG26 13 H2
Ropley Clo. RG26 12 D4
Rosebank Clo. RG26 13 E3
Rosemary Dri. RG26 13 E5
Rotherwick Rd. RG26 13 E5
Rowan Clo. RG26 13 F4
Rowan Rd. RG26 13 F4
St Peters Clo. RG26 12 D5
Sandford Rd. RG26 12 D3
Sandy La. RG26 13 G4
Sarisbury Clo. RG26 12 D4
Sarum Rd. RG26 12 D2
Saunders Gdns. RG26 13 E3
Searing Way. RG26 12 D3
Selbourne Walk. RG26 12 D4
Shaw La. RG26 12 C5
Sheridan Cres. RG26 13 E5
Shyshack La. RG26 12 B2
Silchester Rd. RG26 13 E2
Silverdale Rd. RG26 13 E3
Skates La. RG26 13 F6
Smallwood Dri. RG26 13 E3
Southdown Rd. RG26 12 D3
Spencer Clo. RG26 13 G2
Spiers Clo. RG26 13 F4
Springfield Rd. RG26 13 H2
Stanfield. RG26 13 E3
Stephens Rd. RG26 13 F4
Stokes La. RG26 12 A2
Stratfield Av. RG26 13 F4
Stratfield Ct. RG26 13 F4
Stroud Clo. RG26 13 G2
Swains Clo. RG26 13 E3
Swains Rd. RG26 13 E3
Swanwick Walk. RG26 13 E4
Sympson Rd. RG26 13 G3
Tadley Common Rd.
 RG26 13 F2
Tadley Hill. RG26 13 F2
The Burrows. RG26 12 D2
The Glen. RG26 13 H3
The Green. RG26 13 F5
The Hawthorns. RG26 12 B3
The Lane. RG26 13 E3
The Oaks. RG26 12 D4
The Old Forge. RG26 12 B3
The Orchard. RG26 13 F3
The Warren. RG26 12 D4
Titchfield Clo. RG26 13 E5
Tomlins Clo. RG26 13 E4
Tudor Ct. RG26 13 E3
Tunworth Mews. RG26 13 F4
Turbary Gdns. RG26 13 E2
Valley Way. RG26 13 H2
Vinetree Clo. RG26 13 G4
Violet La. RG26 12 A4
Wakeford Clo. RG26 13 H2
Wakeford Ct. RG26 13 H2
Warblington Clo. RG26 13 F4
Wellington Cres. RG26 12 B3
West St. RG26 13 F3
Westfield Clo. RG26 13 G3
Westlyn Rd. RG26 13 G3
Weyhill Clo. RG26 13 E5
Whitedown Rd. RG26 12 C3
Wickham Clo. RG26 13 E3
Wigmore Rd. RG26 12 C2
Wildmoor Dri. RG26 12 B3
Willow Rd. RG26 13 E4
Winchfield Gdns. RG26 13 E4
Winkworth La. RG26 13 F1
Winston Av. RG26 13 G4
Wolverton Rd. RG26 12 A4

Woodlands Rd. RG26 12 A2

KINGSCLERE

Anchor Rd. RG20 14 C3
Ash Grove. RG20 14 D2
Basingstoke Rd. RG20 14 D2
Bear Hill. RG20 14 B3
Brimley Hill Ct. RG20 14 D2
Brimpton Rd. RG20 14 D2
Bushnells Dri. RG20 14 C2
Byfields Rd. RG20 14 B2
Canons Ct. RG20 14 B2
Cedar Dri. RG20 14 B2
Coppice Rd. RG20 14 D2
Cottington Clo. RG20 14 D2
Ecchinswell Rd. RG20 14 A2
Elm Gro. RG20 14 D2
Elm Grove Farm. RG20 14 D2
Elm Grove Flats. RG20 14 D2
Fawconer Rd. RG20 14 D2
Felden Ct. RG20 14 C3
Fieldgate Dri. RG20 14 B2
Foxs La. RG20 14 D2
Frogs Hole. RG20 14 D2
Garden Clo. RG20 14 D3
Garrett Clo. RG20 14 D2
George St. RG20 14 C2
Greenacre. RG20 14 C2
Greenlands Rd. RG20 14 D2
Hardys Field. RG20 14 B1
Highams Clo. RG20 14 D3
Hollowshot La. RG20 14 B4
Hook Rd. RG20 14 E3
INDUSTRIAL ESTATES:
 Kingsclere Park
 Ind Est. RG20 14 B1
Keeps Mead. RG20 14 B1
Kevin Clo. RG20 14 F3
King John Rd. RG20 14 D3
Knowle Cres. RG20 14 C3
Larch Rd. RG20 14 C3
Link Rd. RG20 14 E2
Longcroft Rd. RG20 14 B1
Love La. RG20 14 C2
Newbury Rd. RG20 14 B1
North St. RG20 14 C2
Peel Gdns. RG20 14 B1
Pennys Hatch. RG20 14 C2
Phoenix Ct. RG20 14 C2
Popes Hill. RG20 14 B2
Poveys Mead. RG20 14 E3
Priors Clo. RG20 14 D2
Queens Rd. RG20 14 B2
Rose Hodson Ct. RG20 14 B2
St Marys Rd. RG20 14 C3
Sandford Clo. RG20 14 F3
South Rd. RG20 14 E2
Strokins Rd. RG20 14 D2
Sunnyside. RG20 14 D2
Swan St. RG20 14 B3
The Dell. RG20 14 D2
The Lines. RG20 14 C1
The Paddock. RG20 14 D2
Thorneley Rd. RG20 14 D2
Tower Hill. RG20 14 B2
Tower Hill Ct. RG20 14 B2
Union La. RG20 14 C1
Wellmans Mdw. RG20 14 B1
Winchester Rd. RG20 14 B4
Yew Clo. RG20 14 E3

OAKLEY

Andover Rd. RG23 15 A2,
Anton Clo. RG23 15 C3
Apple Tree Clo. RG23 15 C5
Arran Clo. RG23 15 C5
Ash Tree Clo. RG23 15 B5
Aviemore Dri. RG23 15 B5
Avon Rd. RG23 15 C3
Barn La. RG23 15 B5
Barra Clo. RG23 15 B2
Beech Tree Clo. RG23 15 C4
Blackwater Clo. RG23 15 C5
Boon Way. RG23 15 B3
Braemar Clo. RG23 15 B3
Cadnam Clo. RG23 15 B3
Caithness Clo. RG23 15 B2
Cedar Tree Clo. RG23 15 C5
Croft Rd. RG23 15 C3
Dellfield. RG23 15 D1
Dever Clo. RG23 15 C3